Making Sense of Good and Evil

Geoffrey Vincent

Copyright © 2020 (Geoffrey Vincent)
All rights reserved worldwide.

No part of this book can be stored, changed, sold, copied or transmitted in any form or by whatever means other than what is outlined in this book without the prior permission in writing of the person holding the copyright, except for the use of brief quotations and certain other non-commercial uses permitted by copyright law.

Note: To avoid any infringement of copyright the author has chosen the King James Bible (KJV) exclusively for comments on Genesis chapters one to six, Mathew 24, Revelations chapters 1 to 22. All other bible quotes are from the New King James Version (NKJV) and King James Bible (KJV).

Publisher: Inspiring Publishers,
P.O. Box 159, Calwell, ACT Australia 2905
Email: publishaspg@gmail.com
http://www.inspiringpublishers.com

 A catalogue record for this book is available from the National Library of Australia

National Library of Australia The Prepublication Data Service

Author: Geoffrey Vincent
Title: Making Sense of Good and Evil
Genre: Non-fiction
ISBN (print): 978-1-922327-52-9
ISBN (eBook): 978-1-922327-53-6

Contents

INTRODUCTION	1
THE GENESIS COMMENTARY	27
- Genesis Chapter 1	27
- Genesis Chapter 2	39
- The Genesis Chronology	47
- Genesis Chapter 3	53
- Genesis Chapter 4	65
- Genesis Chapter 5	77
- Genesis Chapter 6	83
MATTHEW 24	87
THE REVELATION OF JESUS CHRIST	101
- Revelation 1	101
- Revelation 2	111
- Revelation 3	119
- Revelation 4	127
- Revelation 5	133
- Revelation 6	137
- Revelation 7	143
- Revelation 8	147
- Revelation 9	151
- Revelation 10	161
- Revelation 11	165
- Revelation 12	173
- Revelation 13	185
- Revelation 14	195

- Revelation 15 203
- Revelation 16 207
- Revelation 17 213
- Revelation 18 221
- Revelation 19 227
- Revelation 20 233
- Revelation 21 241
- Revelation 22 251

Introduction

What we are witnessing today, especially in the field of technology and medicine, is nothing short of science fiction when one considers that it was only as recent as the 1920's that automobiles surpassed horse and buggy. Those once blind, deaf, and lame, are seeing, hearing, and walking again, thanks to the men and women of science who continue building on the discoveries of those before them. If more of the good news was broadcast we would notice that nations and individuals are performing medical miracles and works of compassion that far outweigh the evil in the world. As science continues to progress with new and exciting breakthroughs, there will always be nurses, doctors, paramedics, fire fighters, police officers, and ordinary everyday citizens who will continue from one generation to the next caring for the communities they serve. Yet with all the advancements in technology and signs of better things to come, many believe we are living in 'the last days'. Are we to believe that everything humanity struggles through with sickness, disease, famine, war, plagues, and so on, is all for nothing?

The greatest obstacle towards world peace is not so much the leaders of the rogue nations but more of the continuing conflicts and wars between the religions that have built their faith on the traditional teaching of a 'fall'. The belief that humanity's woes are due to Adam's sin is held by two and a half billion Catholics and Protestants. Add to that number almost two billion Muslims who also believe that although Adam had sinned, he later realised his mistake and therefore cannot be held responsible for the sins of his offspring. Judaism is of the view we are born in a neutral state and therefore can choose between right and wrong. As it stands today, more than half the world's population of 7.8 billion, as of 2020, are taught that all the evil in the world such as war, famine, sickness, disease, death, and so on, was caused by Adam's sin.

Rarely is a sermon preached without a reminder we are more inclined towards evil rather than good because of an inherent sinful condition. So entrenched is the teaching of original sin that many Christians may find it hard to understand why there are millions upon millions of ordinary everyday people with no knowledge of the bible, yet naturally embrace goodness rather than evil. Genesis and science will never be compatible while creationists ignore what is in plain sight, especially in the fields of archaeology and palaeontology. It is becoming increasingly clear by the day it was very unlikely Adam and Eve were the sole progenitors of the human race.

Most of today's bible scholars are of the opinion that Genesis is just an allegory that explains the origin of evil and therefore should not be taken seriously. However, this line of reasoning puts the gospels in a very precarious position. If the Genesis creation narrative is just an allegory because there appears to be no defence against science, the gospels will also have to be accepted as allegorical seeing that Genesis is the foundation for the gospels teaching. If creationists continue to argue against science, they may also contribute to the irrelevance of the gospels. One of the most difficult challenges in putting forward an alternative view of Genesis in light of science is getting past many of the deep seated beliefs, especially the belief we grow old and die because of a 'fall'. Conversely, to suggest that Adam and Eve were the sole progenitors of the entire human race is one thing, but to suggest that Cain married a sister because there appears to be no other explanation has created more questions than answers, especially since incest is strictly forbidden.

> *Cursed be anyone who lies with his sister, whether the daughter of his father or the daughter of his mother.' And all the people shall say, 'Amen.' (Deuteronomy 27:22).*

Introduction

The traditional teachings of Genesis have caused many to doubt the reliability of the narrative. While it may appear on the surface that Adam and Eve were the sole progenitors of the human race, there is also a parallel narrative that reinforces what science teaches about our origins. Genesis had deliberately held 'a mystery that had been hidden through the ages' until the purpose for what had to be hidden was revealed through the Apostle Paul. The 'mystery' that Paul speaks about in his epistles was not taught by man, but rather a 'revelation' that had changed his entire attitude about keeping the law as a means of righteousness (Galatians 1:11,12). When the truth of Genesis is fully understood, science and religion will no longer be at variance. What first needs to be understood is why the couple that occupied the Garden of Eden played an entirely different role than those commanded to 'be fruitful, multiply, and replenish the earth'. A single man named Adam was formed for a single purpose, and that purpose will be explained in the following commentaries.

When one considers that Adam had only '*become like God, knowing good and evil*' since following Eve into a transgression, it becomes clear why the Apostle Paul states in his letter to Timothy, '*Adam was not deceived*'? (Genesis 3:26. 1 Timothy 2: 14).

Little attention is given to Paul's testimony due to an exegetical misunderstanding of Romans 5:12-21 that appears to put Adam in a very poor light. Paul is no doubt speaking of the '*first* Adam' as a 'type' that introduced the knowledge of sin and death, and the '*last* Adam' as the 'antitype' that held the remedy, yet he does not accuse Adam of actually committing a sin. Paul's use of the Greek word τύπος (typos) is not simply just a 'figure' of something, but the actual original stamp or mark from a blow that is the exact copy of the original. Notice that Paul does not say 'as by one man's *sin*', but rather by 'one man's *disobedience*'.

> *For as by one man's disobedience many were made sinners, so by the obedience of one shall many be made righteous* (Romans 5:19).

To accuse Adam as '*one who sinned*' contradicts Paul's testimony that 'Adam was not deceived' (Romans 5:16. 1Timothy 2:14). (Romans

5:14). That Adam was 'formed and breathed into' by God yet was unaware of what he was doing when following Eve into a transgression defies logic. Before we can even begin to understand what had motivated Adam to disobey the law of the garden; *'thou shalt not'*, we need to understand why the tree of the knowledge of good and evil was planted in the garden in the first place.

Isaiah speaking of the Lord states; *'I form the light, and create darkness: I make peace, and create evil: I the Lord do all these things'* (Isaiah 45:7). Although the above testimony from Isaiah may seem contradictory when compared with the Apostle John's statement *'He that loveth not, knoweth not God; for God is love'*, the point is, without the knowledge of good and evil we would be void of free will and subject to an arbitrary God (1 John 4:8). The very thought of humanity being created in God's 'image and likeness' without the potential to create evil is inconsistent with what the scriptures have to say about the nature of good and evil in relation to our image and likeness of God. So what was the point of creating a world with people who could be murderers, criminals, rapists, and warmongers if an all knowing God was aware there would be consequences due to the knowledge of good and evil? On the other hand, what was the point of creating a world with people who could be compassionate, loving, kind, and gentle, while also having to suffer with sickness, hunger, poverty, war and death? If according to the gospels, the purpose from the beginning was for the Spirit of God to dwell within humanity, is it unreasonable to conclude that if God was willing to dwell within humanity, wouldn't God also have to be willing to share in humanity's suffering and joy?

> *Know ye not that ye are the temple of God, and that the Spirit of God dwelleth in you?"* (1 Corinthians 3:16)

Where scripture speaks of God 'dwelling within', it is speaking about the spirit of God that is within all, whether an agnostic, atheist, or believer. It was the inspiration from 'the spirit within' that Isaiah could say when speaking about God: *'I make peace and I create evil'*. This doesn't mean that God or humanity are evil by nature; it simply means that without the knowledge of good and evil we wouldn't be created in the image and likeness of God. Since we have the freedom to exercise the knowledge of something that is a force for good or evil, there has to be an outcome. According to scripture, if we do good, we belong to God, if we choose evil, we have 'not seen God'.

> *Beloved, follow not that which is evil, but that which is good. He that doeth good is of God: but he that doeth evil hath not seen God* (1 John 1:11).

Law and remedy

Because the knowledge of good and evil is an integral part of our human nature and therefore all may choose between good and evil, there has to be a remedy for wrong doing. If one bible subject is more important than another it is the subject of law and grace. Eve's 'transgression' followed by Adam's 'disobedience', also described by the Apostle Paul as an 'offence', was necessary to teach humanity that law, whether written, spoken, or engraved in stone, cannot change the individual's behaviour or potential to create evil. Eve's transgression was humanity's assurance that through her choice to copulate, the seed to bring *'life and immortality to light through the gospels'* would be revealed in the fullness of time as the remedy to overcome evil (2 Timothy 1:10). The gospels are not based on a rescue plan because of an original sin, but the necessity for God's grace to be revealed due to every person's potential to sin. Eve knew once she had her nakedness revealed, she and her offspring would begin to physically die yet have everlasting life spiritually and physically through procreation of the flesh. Flesh is mere clay, but the spirit is pure, holy, and eternal. Adam was formed as the first *'natural man'* for the purpose of his seed bringing immortality to light through the last *'spiritual man'*.

> *Howbeit that was not first which is spiritual, but that which is natural; and afterward that which is spiritual* (1 Corinthians 15:46).

Eve may well have resisted the temptation of partaking from the tree of knowledge of good and evil and therefore have remained innocent of her nakedness and remained childless. 'The tree of life' mentioned first in Genesis and again in the final chapter of the bible, remains the symbol of everlasting life through each family tree. Therefore the tree of the knowledge of good and evil and the tree of life go hand in hand. There would be no point in a tree of life without the knowledge of good and evil. It was not the tree of life that was guarded once Adam and Eve were expelled, but rather 'the *way* of the tree of life' (Genesis 3:24). The 'way' of the tree of life meant that had Adam and Eve chose to forever partake from the tree of life they would have remained immortal and without offspring. If the Garden of Eden was the original place where procreation was to begin, there would have been no need for the couple to be 'afraid' or to 'hide' themselves (Genesis 3:24. 3:7-10).

To simply accept those described as 'male and female' and commanded to *'be fruitful, multiply, and replenish the earth'* refer to Adam and Eve contradicts the overall narrative. By not considering Eve's transition from sexual innocence to sexual awareness ignores the obvious. Had Eve had any desire to procreate, she would not have needed any prompting to have her eyes opened to her nakedness. Eve's decision to procreate knowing she would grow old and die was an act of unselfishness. Rather than living a meaningless existence without offspring, Eve knew that life outside of Eden would be much more meaningful and aware that her offspring were not without hope despite the knowledge of evil. The hope and assurance that Eve had, was the promise that would come to pass through the seed that was to bring life and immortality to light through the gospel.

The first and last Adam.

It is essential to understand why the first Adam as a 'type' is named in Luke's gospel as the Son of God, and why the last Adam as the 'antitype'. is also named the Son of God. There can only be one Son of God. Mathew likely would not have exalted Adam as the son of

Introduction

God if he was guilty of sin. Notice the final conclusion of Mathew's genealogy back from Jesus[1] to Adam.

Which was the son of Enos, which was the son of Seth, which was the son of Adam, which was the son of God (Luke 3:38).

The New Testament speaks about the Son of God as *'the author and finisher of our faith'*, *'the alpha and the omega of God'*, 'the *beginning and the end'*, *'the first and the last'* (Hebrews 12:2. Revelation 22:13). Genesis calls our attention to *'the beginning of the creation of God'* when the Spirit of God was breathed into the first natural man (Revelation 3:14). When Jesus had uttered those final words *'It is finished'*, the *omega* of God had completed what the *alpha* of God had begun. What was breathed into the first Adam was *the beginning of the creation of God* within the flesh and blood of humanity (Revelation 3:14). The first natural man and last spiritual man ensured that the fullness of God would forever dwell within humanity (1 Corinthians 3:16).

Adam's deliberate 'disobedience' was an 'offence' necessary to reveal God's grace, but not without a price. The last Adam nailed the curse of the law to the cross for all who would fall short of keeping the law. On Calvary's cross the beauty of the serpent symbol was revealed. The figurative serpent that introduced the knowledge of evil was the same figurative serpent that held the remedy for the venom of sin. The following commentaries from Genesis chapters two and three will explain why it could only be Adam who could reason with Eve for the sake of redeeming all who would succumb to the pleasures of the flesh, and only Adam who could bring both flesh and spirit together as one new person.

Moses had fashioned a 'bronze serpent' and elevated it on a pole as a symbol for the remedy for those bitten by venomous serpents while in the 'wilderness of sin' (Numbers 21: 6-9). The serpent in

---
[1] Jesus correct Hebrew name is Yeshua - a shortened name from the Hebrew Yehoshua meaning God is salvation. The Greek New Testament transliteration from Yehoshua to *Iesous* was later translated into the Latin *Iesus*. As the result of the Norman invasion of England in the 11th century, the letter 'J' eventually replaced first male names starting with 'I' or 'Y' because 'J' had more of a masculine sound: hence names like Iames or Iakob became James and Jacob. The name *Jesus* therefore does not reflect the true sense of the Hebrew meaning *God is salvation*. However, to avoid any confusion, the author has chosen to use the name 'Jesus'.

the wilderness was the precursor that symbolized the last Adam's admission that because he introduced the knowledge of good and evil he was therefore willing to bear the responsibility, not for sin itself, but for those infected by the venom of sin. Who other but the one who introduced humanity to the knowledge of good and evil could willingly be a symbolic 'serpent'?

> *And as Moses lifted up the serpent in the wilderness, even so must the Son of man be lifted up* (John 3:14).

The whole purpose of 'the last Adam', submitting to the humiliation and shame of being crucified was to 'condemn sin in the flesh' so a new spiritual *body* would be free from the curse of law. Only the last Adam could be the remedy for what the first Adam had introduced. God's grace was necessary for the healing of the knowledge of sin and death.

> *For what the law could not do, in that it was weak through the flesh, God sending his own Son in the likeness of sinful flesh, and for sin, condemned sin in the flesh: That the righteousness of the law might be fulfilled in us, who walk not after the flesh, but after the Spirit* (Romans 8:3,4).

The only possibility for the Creator to dwell within humanity for the sake of his church, was to manifest a Son that would condemn sin in the flesh. The newly formed 'body of Christ', referred to by the Apostle Paul as 'the Church' had marked the beginning and construction of a spiritual temple where God could now dwell without the necessity for moral laws written on stone tablets that explicitly state 'you shall not'.

> *Knowing this, that the law is not made for a righteous man, but for the lawless and disobedient, for the ungodly and for sinners, for unholy and profane, for murderers of fathers and murderers of mothers, for manslayers* (1 Timothy 1:9).

Jesus' message about justice and mercy fell on deaf ears. Although those two words are opposites, they are related. The law demands justice, but justice related to Mosaic Law requires grace wherever grace is warranted.

Introduction

Moreover the law entered, that the offence might abound. But where sin abounded, grace did much more abound (Romans 5:20).

Although Jesus had forgiven and pardoned a certain woman caught in adultery, the law keepers would have preferred to stone her to death, but when Jesus pointed out the sins of those who had accused her, they quickly had a change of heart.

When Jesus had lifted up himself, and saw none but the woman, he said unto her, Woman, where are those thine accusers? hath no man condemned thee? She said, No man, Lord. And Jesus said unto her, Neither do I condemn thee: go, and sin no more (John 8:10, 11).

Jerusalem had eventually become a stronghold for everything governed by law. Mercy and forgiveness came with a price. Its economy, religion, and central place of worship were based on rules and regulations becoming more and more burdensome. To this day, although the penalty for breaking the law is the only means of deterring bad behaviour, law is not without its faults, especially civil law. Judges have their hands tied, evident where the punishment does not fit the crime. It is now at the point where no one is safe under 'the rule of law'. Western civilization is eroding to where ordinary everyday people are becoming increasingly disturbed with the unfairness handed down by judges. If parents cannot teach offspring from an early age the value of ethical behaviour based on decent family values, secular leaders may have no other choice but to reintroduce the Ten Commandments into primary schools as a guide for good behaviour. Enforcing moral law may sound irrational, but if children raised under Muslim Law prove to behave better than non-Muslims, secular governments may have no choice but to join hands with Christian leaders and reintroduce the Ten Commandments. However, history proves that moral law whether Muslim or Christian, has done nothing to stop violence, unrest, wars and conflicts between those two religions or any other religion that uses law to discourage bad behaviour.

The redundancy of law

The Apostle Paul insists that when we bear each other's burdens all written laws are redundant.

> *Bear ye one another's burdens, and so fulfil the law of Christ* (Galatians 6:2).

This all important teaching of 'the law of Christ' is misunderstood because very few understand the true meaning of Christ. The Apostle Paul's statement; *'But you have not so learned Christ'* is at the heart of his teaching (Ephesians 4:20). Had Paul said 'you have not so learned Hebrew or Greek', his statement would have been easier to understand, but to say that Christ is something to be 'learned' is not so easy to identify with. While we continue to argue whether Jesus, Mohammad, Buddha, or any other sage or prophet has the truth, there will never be unity until the knowledge of Christ is re-established. There is much confusion about the Word of God and the connection between Jesus, God, the Holy Spirit, and the Christ of God.

By way of a simple explanation, Christ is not a person, but rather the Logos of God that is the divine reasoning from where humanity's goodness, creativity, and intelligence spring. In other words, the Logos of God is 'the Word that was with God and was God (John 1:1). The Word of God is not a person. There is a difference between Jesus the man who was born 'according to the flesh' and 'the fullness of Christ' that was within the man (Romans 1:3). In every instance where Jesus is mentioned ahead of Christ, as in 'Jesus Christ', the emphasis is on the man Jesus as one proclaiming the message of the Kingdom of God. But whenever Christ is mentioned ahead of Jesus, as in 'Christ Jesus', the emphasis is on the title before the name to distinguish the fullness of the Word of God that was within the person of Jesus. Where 'Christ' is used singularly, Christ relates to the Word of God that now dwells within humanity. It is 'Christ within' that is humanity's hope of glory, not an external god or gods (Colossians 1:27). Note the following from the Apostle Paul.

But the righteousness of faith speaks in this way, "Do not say in your heart, 'Who will ascend into heaven?' " (that is, to bring Christ down from above) or, " 'Who will descend into the abyss?' " (that is, to bring Christ up from the dead). But what does it say? "The word is near you, in your mouth and in your heart" (that is, the word of faith which we preach): (Romans 10:6-8).

Christ is the unifying principle that will bring humanity together as one body of faith. The enforcement of law cannot work because the very nature of judicial law is opposed to the knowledge and meaning of *Christ, 'the end of the law for righteousness'* (Romans 10:4). The Apostle Paul's admonition about 'learning Christ' is to understand the meaning of having the mind of Christ.

Let this mind be in you, which was 'also' in Christ Jesus: (Philippians 2:5).

The mind of Christ

But what does it mean to 'also' have the mind of Christ Jesus? That question is best explained by asking what is in the mind of paramedics, police officers, firemen, nurses, teachers, believers, agnostics, or any ordinary everyday person regardless of gender, race or colour, who will risk his or her own life to save a stranger.

Greater love hath no man than this, that a man lay down his life for his friends (John 15:13).

What is in the mind of an atheist who can show love and compassion and a deep sense of grief for his or her neighbour or friend when they lose everything through fire, flood, accident, sickness, or any other unexpected tragedy? Whether believer, agnostic, or atheist, we each have an inherent sense of oneness that naturally springs into action, especially in times of tragedy. Religion does not have a monopoly on righteousness.

There is neither Greek nor Jew, circumcision nor uncircumcision, Barbarian, Scythian, bond nor free: but Christ is all, and in all (Colossians 3:11).

It is the Christ principle, whether believer or unbeliever that draws us together in times of need. Paul's 'revelation of Jesus Christ' was the turning point in his understanding of what it means to be Christ minded.

> *But I certify you, brethren that the Gospel which was preached of me is not after man. For I neither received it of man, neither was I taught it, but by the revelation of Jesus Christ* (Galatians 1:11, 12).

Christ is 'the Word that was from the beginning'. It is 'Christ within' that enables humanity to have compassion for the poor, hungry, sick, and so on. 'The word that is near you' enables men and women of science to help the blind to see, the lame to walk, the deaf to hear. It is not the spirit and mind of man alone, but the omniscient word that dwells within humanity. We are only just beginning to see medical miracles from men and women of science who are doing their best to discover cures for sickness, pain, and suffering. Christ is the omniscient indwelling within humanity that is bringing immortality to light. Christ within is the 'hope of glory' by which the Apostle Paul could confidently say:

> *'But as it is written, Eye hath not seen, nor ear heard, neither have entered into the heart of man, the things which God hath prepared for them that love him* (1 Corinthians 2:9).

Paul is not speaking about things outside of this world but things within this world being prepared for those that love God. 'Learning Christ' may sound unusual, but with an understanding of what 'the risen body of Christ' stands for, the meaning of Christ's death and resurrection takes on a whole new meaning. The 'body of Christ' is not a physical earthly body with members answerable to men, but a spiritual body with members of Christ from all nations regardless of colour, gender, or race, answerable only to God.

> *Who now rejoice in my sufferings for you, and fill up that which is behind of the afflictions of Christ in my flesh for his body's sake, which is the church* (Colossians 1:24).

Paul affirms that the body and members of Christ remain in this world forever; Notice the following;

> *That there should be no schism in the body; but that the members should have the same care one for another. And whether one member suffers, all the members suffer with it; or one member be honoured, all the members rejoice with it. Now ye are the body of Christ, and members in particular. (1 Corinthians 12:25-27).Unto him be glory in the church by Christ Jesus throughout all ages, world without end. Amen* (Ephesians 3:21).

Although the Apostle Paul refers to our state of consciousness in terms of 'alive to Christ', 'asleep in Christ', or 'dead in Christ', most of Paul's statements are interpreted literally rather than spiritually. For example, the 'dead in Christ' has nothing to do with people literally dead, but rather a state of mind. The mind that is 'alive to Christ' speaks of goodness, peace, compassion, truth, justice, and so on, while those 'dead in Christ' speak the opposite. Many who are 'asleep in Christ' are often 'awakened' through personal tragedies and circumstances that draw communities nearer to God. According to Jesus, all who are peacemakers, merciful, pure in heart, compassionate, are 'children of God', the 'salt of the earth', and a 'light to the world'. Mathew Chapter 5 excellently describes ordinary, everyday people as living examples of those with the mind of Christ Jesus (refer to Mathew 5:5-16).

The Christ principle.

The writers of antiquity described *logos* as the divine reason that had set in motion the creative order of the cosmos. The logos or Word of God according to the scriptures is the Christ principle that was 'with' God and 'was' God. The Gospel of John states;

> *'In the beginning was the Word, and the Word was with God, and the Word was God'* (John 1:1).

The Word is not a person but rather something unseen yet evident by what can be seen (Romans 1:20). 'God' is the all-encompassing 'everything' that brought the universe into existence from out of nothing. When the bible speaks of the 'Godhead', it is not referring to separate gods, but One God.

> *There is one body and one Spirit, just as you were called in one hope of your calling; one Lord, one faith, one baptism; one God and Father of all, who is above all, and through all, and in you all* (Ephesians 4:4,5).

Whether the scriptures speak of God, Christ, Logos, Word of God, Holy Spirit, all are the ONE divine principle that brought all living things into existence.

> *Where there is neither Greek nor Jew, circumcision nor uncircumcision, Barbarian, Scythian, bond nor free: but Christ is all, and in all* (Colossians 3:11).

The forgotten Christ.

When Christians had formally merged with political Rome into *'one holy catholic and apostolic Church'*, it was hoped that the knowledge of Christ would be forgotten. It was a time that saw a well orchestrated transformation of power that was the saving grace of the Roman Empire. What is assumed by many historians as 'the fall of Rome' was nothing more than transferring power in a different guise. Had the church fathers stood their ground and refused to sign what many believed had contradicted the scriptures about Christ, there may have been less reason for Mohammad or any other prophet to have a reason to start a new religion. Had the knowledge of Christ not been lost, there would have been no need for a Protestant Reformation let alone the rise of hundreds of protestant cults and sects that remain to this day.

Neither Jesus nor the Apostles alluded to anything that even resembles a 'church creed'. The first ecumenical council of 325 C.E. clarified the nature of Jesus Christ to counteract the Arian doctrine that Christ was not divine but rather a created being. Following the first council of Nicaea, the second council of Constantinople in 381 C.E. clarified the definition of the Father, Son, and the Holy

Spirit to what is accepted today as the 'Trinity'. What followed were centuries of unspeakable horrors. A simple faith once based on Jesus' teachings of love and compassion had become a religion that meted out punishment, persecution, torment, and death to anyone who would not conform to her doctrines and beliefs.

Although many of today's contemporary scholars question the wording of the creed as it relates to the nature of Jesus and his manner of birth, it is unlikely that the nature of Christ will be questioned, for fear of destabilizing the very foundation of Judaic Christianity as we know it today. Before examining whether Christianity's official creed reflects the biblical testimony on the nature of Christ and what constitutes 'one holy catholic and apostolic church' as opposed to the true meaning of 'church', observe the wording of the official church creed:

Nicene Creed

We believe in one God, the Father, the Almighty, maker of heaven and earth, of all that is, seen and unseen. We believe in one Lord, Jesus Christ, the only Son of God, eternally begotten of the Father, God from God, Light from Light, true God from true God, begotten, not made, of one Being with the Father. Through him all things were made. For us and for our salvation he came down from heaven: by the power of the Holy Spirit he became incarnate from the Virgin Mary, and was made man. For our sake he was crucified under Pontius Pilate; he suffered death and was buried. On the third day he rose again in accordance with the Scriptures; he ascended into heaven and is seated at the right hand of the Father. He will come again in glory to judge the living and the dead, and his kingdom will have no end. We believe in the Holy Spirit, the Lord, the giver of life, who proceeds from the Father and the Son. With the Father and the Son he is worshiped and glorified. He has spoken through the Prophets. We believe in one holy catholic and apostolic Church. We acknowledge one baptism for the forgiveness of sins. We look for the resurrection of the dead, and the life of the world to come.

While the creed is crystal clear that only after Jesus returns will the Kingdom of God have no end, the Apostle Paul states the opposite;

> *'Unto him be glory in the church by Christ Jesus throughout all ages, world without end. Amen* (Ephesians 3:21).

Since the true meaning of 'church' had been misrepresented, most Christians would disagree that Paul is talking about a permanent and unbroken kingdom set up in Jesus' time. Many think of 'church' as a physical building of wood and stone where communities gather for worship, marriage ceremonies, funerals, and so on, rather than 'church' as a universal spiritual body.

The hundreds of 'churches' representing various branches of Christianity is a testimony to how the meaning of church has been lost. Rather than describe the 'body of Christ' for what it is, the church creed substitutes the spiritual body of Christ to suit its own ends. The distorted view of the true church had stripped believers of the freedom they once shared in the knowledge of Christ.

> *And hath put all things under his feet, and gave him to be the head over all things to the church, Which is his body, the fulness of him that fills all in all* (Ephesians 1:22, 23).

The Apostle Paul had warned his followers of a counterfeit church that ultimately ruled under its own laws and regulations by setting up its own holy place from where an earthly representative would administer power and authority over all ecclesiastical matters.

> *Let no man deceive you by any means: for that day shall not come, except there come a falling away first, and that man of sin be revealed, the son of perdition; Who opposeth and exalteth himself above all that is called God, or that is worshipped; so that he as God sitteth in the temple of God, shewing himself that he is God* (2 Thessalonians 2:2,3).

The Nicene Creed not only omits the relevance of the body of Christ as what constitutes the true 'church', but also distorts the truth about who was responsible for crucifying the Christ. The creed states that Jesus suffered under Pontius Pilate, yet according to the plain and simple testimony from scripture, Pilate wanted Jesus immediately released. Notice Peter's condemnation of Israel's role in Jesus crucifixion;

> *Ye men of Israel, hear these words; Jesus of Nazareth, a man approved of God among you by miracles and wonders and signs, which God did by him in the midst of you, as ye yourselves also know: Him, being delivered by the determinate counsel and foreknowledge of God, ye have taken, and by wicked hands have crucified and slain* (Acts 2:22,23).

The 'wicked hands' were certainly not the hands of the Romans, but the religious leaders who plotted Jesus' death. Jesus was not only persecuted because of his differences with the Pharisees, but also because he was a threat to the Jewish economy. The only way to disguise the Pharisees true motive for wanting to have Jesus crucified was to have him charged for blasphemy. However it is clear that Pontius Pilate wanted no part of it.

> *Pilate therefore, willing to release Jesus, spake again to them. But they cried, saying, Crucify him, crucify him. And he said unto them the third time, Why, what evil hath he done? I have found no cause of death in him: I will therefore chastise him, and let him go. And they were instant with loud voices, requiring that he might be crucified. And the voices of them and of the chief priests prevailed. And Pilate gave sentence that it should be as they required* (Luke 23:20-24).

Pilate could find no reason to have Jesus put to death. Although he washed his hands of the matter in front of the whole multitude, he nevertheless had to comply with Jewish Sanhedrin Law as a matter of political expediency (Mathew 27:24). The Nicene Creed had cleverly laid the blame solely on Pontius Pilate to distract from their real motive. Had the Nicene Creed stated that Jesus was crucified under the authority of the Jewish high priest Caiaphas, the Jewish religious leaders of the day would have taken exception, and for a very good reason. The term 'Judeo - Christianity' first coined at the beginning of the 19th century, represents the religion that was initially Judaic and based on law. 'The one holy catholic and apostolic church' was clever enough not to mention anything about 'Christ as the end of the law for righteousness' or that 'Christ within is the hope of glory', or the true meaning of 'church' because of the Jews disagreement about the nature of Christ. Instead, 'the one holy catholic and apostolic church' continues to hold to the Ten Commandments as the guide to righteousness.

Although the deliberate fabrication within the wording of the official church creed has undermined the meaning of Christ, no doubt there are many 'Christ minded' Catholics, Protestants, Jews, Hindus, Buddhists, popes, bishops, believers, unbelievers, agnostics, that are 'Christ minded' regardless of their beliefs.

Anti-Christ

The correct rendering of the Greek word 'antichrist' (αντίχριστος) literally means 'instead of Christ' or 'in place of Christ'. Antichrist has a twofold meaning; one that symbolizes the political powers that enforce civil law to discourage bad behaviour, the other, the religious powers that subject believers to church law, creeds, and 'doctrines of men' as a means of good behaviour. If there is to be a shared belief that can bring humanity together as one body of Christ, it is unlikely that such a transition will begin until the knowledge of Christ is reclaimed and individuals can begin to think for themselves.

Regardless of whether religious or civil, all laws are mere shadows of the substance. 'The mind of Christ' is our God given consciousness that gives every individual the free will to discern between good and evil (2 Thessalonians 2:1-12). The Apostle Paul speaks about Christ as *'a mystery which has been hidden from ages and from generations, but now has been revealed to His saints'* (Colossians 1:26). Had the knowledge of Christ not been 'hidden through the ages', the seed that was to bring the Christ child into the world would no doubt have been in danger, hence the parallel narrative of Genesis that veils the origin of Christ. When Herod heard of a rumour that the Christ child was born, he immediately set out to murder every Jewish infant that was a potential threat to his power. However, the promised seed not only survived, but continues to bear fruit to this day. The preservation of the seed was 'hidden' within the descendants of Adam, through to Abraham, David, and finally Joseph. While the language and symbolism of the Old and New Testaments may give the impression of things yet to come, we are admonished by Paul to discern between what is literal and what is spiritual. As the Apostle Paul states;

> *But the natural man receiveth not the things of the Spirit of God: for they are foolishness unto him: neither can he know them, because they are spiritually discerned* (1 Corinthians 2:14).

The New Jerusalem

As an example, very few had understood what Jesus had meant by 'destroy this temple, and in three days I will raise it up' (John 2:19). Many were offended by his words because they thought Jesus was speaking about the destruction of Herod's temple when Jesus had said:

> *In my Father's house are many mansions: if it were not so, I would have told you. I go to prepare a place for you* (John 14:2).

Jesus was not speaking about a huge physical mansion with smaller dwellings within, somewhere out in the universe, but a single spiritual temple within this world with members of 'the body of Christ' representing one temple of God. (1 Corinthians 3:16-17).

> *And I saw a new heaven and a new earth: for the first heaven and the first earth were passed away; and there was no more sea. And I John saw the holy city, New Jerusalem, coming down from God out of heaven, prepared as a bride adorned for her husband. And I heard a great voice out of heaven saying, Behold, the tabernacle of God is with men, and he will dwell with them, and they shall be his people, and God himself shall be with them, and be their God* (Revelation 21:1-3).

While it may appear that the New Jerusalem is a physical city literally going to descend from the heavens, notice the following testimony.

> *But you have come to Mount Zion and to the city of the living God, the heavenly Jerusalem, to an innumerable company of angels, to the general assembly and church of the firstborn who are registered in heaven, to God the Judge of all, to the spirits of just men made perfect* (Hebrews 12:22, 23).

Regrettably, the 'body of Christ' is no longer understood as something permanently established in this world. There is a need to discern where and when the language of the New Testament needs to be rightly divided between what is natural and what is spiritual (2 Timothy 2:15). There can only be one faith and one baptism, therefore one united 'body in Christ' (Ephesians 4:5). The members of the body of Christ are not divided. We are figuratively inside or outside the New Jerusalem. Meanwhile, the hundreds of branches of Christianity that continue to argue whether Jesus will return before, during, or after an apocalypse, need to rethink about the meaning of the Kingdom of God, when it was established, and why it is permanently here on earth.

When the Apostle Peter addressed those gathered at Pentecost confused about what had occurred, he put to rest any doubt about the Old Testament prophecies concerning 'the last days'. Although Peter explained that what the congregation had witnessed was the fulfilment of Joel's prophecy, many today are not convinced and would rather believe that Joel's prophecy was only partly fulfilled at Pentecost. Notice Peter's discourse on Joel's unmistakable description of 'the last days'.

> *But this is that which was spoken by the prophet Joel; And it shall come to pass in the last days, saith God, I will pour out of my Spirit upon all flesh: and your sons and your daughters shall prophesy, and your young men shall see visions, and your old men shall dream dreams: And on my servants and on my handmaidens I will pour out in those days of my Spirit; and they shall prophesy: And I will shew wonders in heaven above, and signs in the earth beneath; blood, and fire, and vapour of smoke: The sun shall be turned into darkness, and the moon into blood, before the great and notable day of the Lord come:* (Acts 2:17-20).

'Wonders in the heavens above', 'signs in the earth beneath', 'blood fire and vapour of smoke', 'the sun turning to darkness and moon turning to blood' are figurative expressions of the new age that had arrived in the 1st century A.D. Perceiving things as purely literal is likened by Paul as one drinking the 'milk of the word', while those who discern what is spiritual are ready to digest the 'meat of the word'.

> *For when for the time ye ought to be teachers, ye have need that one teach you again which be the first principles of the oracles of God; and are become such as have need of milk, and not of strong meat.* (Hebrews 5:12).

The end of religion

Many figurative descriptions of the New Testament are repeats from the Old Testament that describe the impending doom of Israel because of her figurative 'adulteries'. It should be mentioned that although the Jews to this day are despised by many individuals and nations of the world, it was only because of their rejection of Jesus that the Gentiles have been blessed with the Gospel of Christ (Romans 11:11,12). It is also worth noting that the seed that had brought life and immortality to light through the gospel was only made possible through the nation of Israel (2 Timothy 1:10). Here we have a parallel message about Eve's transgression and Israel's transgression. Whereas Eve's transgression was for humanity's blessing in learning about law and grace, Israel's transgressions saw the curse of the law nailed to the cross for the Gentiles not making the same mistake. Within the narratives of Eve's transgression and Israel's transgressions is a glimpse of why Isaiah could say; *'I, the Lord create evil'* (Isaiah 45:7). Sometimes evil is necessary for the outworking of good. Life is a tapestry of mysteries that somehow makes sense, especially when good is born from out of evil. Nations of the world will never be grateful for Israel's rejection of Christ until the world understands why their sacrifices were necessary for the good of humanity. Notice just one of many examples from the Old Testament prophets that describe Israel's defiance and rebelliousness against God.

> *The LORD said also unto me in the days of Josiah the king, Hast thou seen that which backsliding Israel hath done? she is gone up upon every high mountain and under every green tree, and there hath played the harlot. And I said after she had done all these things, Turn thou unto me. But she returned not. And her treacherous sister Judah saw it. And I saw, when for all the causes whereby backsliding Israel committed adultery I had put her away, and given her a bill of divorce; yet her treacherous sister Judah feared not, but went and played the harlot also. And it came to pass through the lightness of her whoredom, that she defiled the land, and committed adultery with stones and with stocks. And yet for all this her treacherous sister Judah hath not turned unto me with her whole heart, but feignedly, saith the LORD* (Jeremiah 3:6-10).

The Old Testament prophets such as Ezekiel, Daniel, Jeremiah, Isaiah, and the Minor Prophets from Hosea to Malachi, speak of Israel and Judah in language that describes Israel's unfaithfulness. To say that Israel was not at the centre of 'God's vengeance' is to ignore its history of backsliding and continuous rejection of the prophets. Jesus displayed his own frustration and righteous indignation when he upturned the tables of the money changers operating their places of business within the temple walls. The Pharisees were determined to get rid of Jesus and his teachings from the time he exposed their hypocrisies. Jerusalem had figuratively become like Babylon of old, thus Jerusalem is described as 'Babylon the Great, the Mother of Harlots'. That may sound very judgmental and unfair to the Jewish religion, but the teaching of the Ten Commandments as the sinners guide to righteousness is the legacy because of their ignorance of Christ. The very name 'Judaic Christianity' speaks for itself. The figurative 'Mother of Harlots' spoken of in Revelations was the union of Judaic law and Christianity and the eventual hundreds of offshoots symbolised as 'daughters' of a religion that claims to be 'one holy catholic and apostolic Church' that upholds law as a guide to righteousness.

When the physical city of Jerusalem was destroyed almost two thousand years ago, the figurative New Jerusalem was raised from the ashes and remains to this day as an eternal spiritual city where ordinary everyday people are called to 'come out of Babylon'. Any religion based on fundamental rules and regulations is anti-Christ. According to the Book of Revelations, the members of the body of Christ are figuratively described as 'undefiled' because they are symbolically clothed in 'white raiment', a covering that represents 'the righteousness of Christ'. John's visions describe the members of the body of Christ wearing symbolic robes of righteousness because of their faith. They are redeemed not because of their own righteousness, but because of the righteousness of Christ imputed to them because of their faith. The events before and in the aftermath of the destruction of Jerusalem marked the 'end of the world' and beginning of a new age. Notice the similarities between the Old Testament descriptions of Israel and the New Testament meaning of 'Babylon'. (The following commentary on 'The Book of the Revelation of Jesus Christ' will explain more about the meaning of the figurative language).

And another angel, a second one, followed, saying, "Fallen, fallen is Babylon the great, she who has made all the nations drink of the wine of the passion of her immorality (Revelation 14:8).

The great city was split into three parts, and the cities of the nations fell. Babylon the great was remembered before God, to give her the cup of the wine of His fierce wrath (Revelation 16:19).

Then one of the seven angels who had the seven bowls came and spoke with me, saying, "Come here, I will show you the judgment of the great harlot who sits on many waters, with whom the kings of the earth committed acts of immorality, and those who dwell on the earth were made drunk with the wine of her immorality. And he carried me away in the Spirit into a wilderness; and I saw a woman sitting on a scarlet beast, full of blasphemous names, having seven heads and ten horns. The woman was clothed in purple and scarlet, and adorned with gold and precious stones and pearls, having in her hand a gold cup full of abominations and of the unclean things of her immorality, and on her forehead a name was written, a mystery, "BABYLON THE GREAT, THE MOTHER OF HARLOTS AND OF THE ABOMINATIONS OF THE EARTH." *And I saw the woman drunk with the blood of the saints, and with the blood of the witnesses of Jesus. When I saw her, I wondered greatly* (Revelation 17:1-6).

The end of the world

It was an earth shattering experience when the Romans destroyed the old city of Jerusalem. The Jew's final rejection of Jesus was a pivotal point in history that saw the end of a religion at the centre of the old city of Jerusalem that had subjected believers to bondage and fear. It was a day of vengeance and retribution, not only because they had rejected Jesus, the last of the prophets, but also retribution for all the previous prophets sent to warn her of an impending judgment. It is a mistake to interpret 'the end of the world' as something yet to be fulfilled. Jesus had warned Israel forty years previously;

> *For then shall be great tribulation, such as was not since the beginning of the world to this time, no, nor ever shall be* (Mathew 24:21).

> *And Jesus said unto them, See ye not all these things? verily I say unto you, There shall not be left here one stone upon another, that shall not be thrown down. And as he sat upon the mount of Olives, the disciples came unto him privately, saying, Tell us, when shall these things be? and what shall be the sign of thy coming, and of the end of the world?* (Mathew 24:2, 3)

Jesus had used many metaphors when describing the destruction of Jerusalem and the aftershock in terms such as 'earthquake', 'lightning shining from east to west', 'the sun being darkened' 'the moon no longer giving light', with similar metaphors used in John's visions. Unfortunately many sects and cults that had sprung from the reformation use those metaphors to fit with their interpretations of past events and apocalyptic future events. However, when John's visions are understood in light of the body of Christ as it relates to the early church, the visions are a 'blessing' to all who read and understand. Note the wording to the introduction to the Revelation of Jesus Christ;

> *Blessed is he who reads and those who hear the words of this prophecy, and keep those things which are written in it; for the time is near* (Revelation 1:3).

We are now living in a new dispensation of time. Jesus' teaching of the Kingdom of God was not about a future paradise, but where each of us may find paradise within this world.

> *And when he was demanded of the Pharisees, when the kingdom of God should come, he answered them and said, The kingdom of God cometh not with observation: Neither shall they say, Lo here! or, lo there! for, behold, the kingdom of God is within you* (Luke 17:20,21).

The first two verses of the epistle named 'Hebrews' clearly states;

> *God, who at sundry times and in divers manners spake in time past unto the fathers by the prophets, hath in these last days spoken unto us by his Son, whom he hath appointed heir of all things, by whom also he made the worlds* (Hebrews 1:1,2).

Almost the entire New Testament addresses things relating to the present. Notice the following;

> *The Revelation of Jesus Christ, which God gave unto him, to shew unto his servants things which must shortly come to pass; and he sent and signified it by his angel unto his servant* (Revelation 1:1).

> *And he said unto me, These sayings are faithful and true: and the Lord God of the holy prophets sent his angel to shew unto his servants the things which must shortly be done. (Revelation 22:6).*

> *Behold, I come quickly: blessed is he that keepeth the sayings of the prophecy of this book* (Revelation 22:7).

> *Behold, I come quickly: hold that fast which thou hast, that no man take thy crown* (Revelation 3:11).

And he saith unto me, Seal not the sayings of the prophecy of this book: for the time is at hand (Revelation 22:10).

And, behold, I come quickly; and my reward is with me, to give every man according as his work shall be (Revelation 22:12)

If this world was to end in a holocaust, the Gospel of Christ wouldn't be described as 'good news'. Hopefully the following commentaries will make more sense of Genesis and the Gospel's narratives that will help the reader understand what the scriptures truly teach about 'the end of the world'. The following commentaries from Matthew 24 is an introduction to the Book of Revelations that explains how,when,and why, the world had ended almost two thousand years ago.

The Genesis Commentary
Genesis Chapter 1

Day 1

1:1   In the beginning God created the heaven and the earth.

Both Genesis and the gospels express simple yet profound matter-of-fact statements which bid the reader to believe or disbelieve as though one is predisposed to faith or unbelief. The Bible's shortest definition of God is found in the Gospel of John: *'God is love, and he who abides in love abides in God and God in him'* (1 John 4:16). While nonbelievers deny the existence of God and believers defend the existence of God, neither can deny that love is an existential experience. Whether we embrace love or are torn apart by the pain of it, we cannot deny that 'love is'.

Although the Hebrew word for God (אלוהים Elohim) may refer to several gods, Elohim is the God of all other gods as far as the writers of the Old Testament are concerned. Elohim in its dual form is introduced here to reveal exactly when the interaction between the figurative 'Father and Son' had begun. The traditional teaching that the Word had become flesh and dwelt amongst us thousands of years after what was assumed to be 'a fall', contradicts what Genesis reveals about the identity of 'us' later in verse twenty six and explained further in chapter two.

1:2   And the earth was without form, and void; and darkness was upon the face of the deep. And the Spirit of God moved upon the face of the waters.

1:3   And God said, Let there be light: and there was light.

1:4   And God saw the light, that it was good: and God divided the light from the darkness.

1:5   And God called the light Day, and the darkness he called Night. And the evening and the morning were the first day.

There is no explanation about the origin of the 'Spirit of God', nor the magnitude of what was meant by 'God said'. The first three verses of Genesis distinguish between God and Spirit, yet so far there is no mention of the Word of God, the Christ of God, the Holy Ghost, or the Son of God. The New Testament describes God as the Word (logos) that 'was' and 'is' one with God: Not until the Gospel of John was written do we find references to those terms.

In the beginning was the Word, and the Word was with God, and the Word was God. The same was in the beginning with God. All things were made by him; and without him was not anything made that was made. In him was life; and the life was the light of men. And the light shineth in darkness; and the darkness comprehended it not (John 1:1-5).

And the Word was made flesh, and dwelt among us, (and we beheld his glory, the glory as of the only begotten of the Father,) full of grace and truth (John 1:14).

John's New Testament gospel is clear that the Word, otherwise described as the logos, *was* and *is* all that encompasses the Elohim. In Greek philosophy, 'logos' was defined as the 'divine reason'. The Spirit of God moved upon the face of the waters from where the Word was active in transforming the chaos into what would become a functional living world. The Hebrew word for Spirit (חרוּן pronounced we-ru-ah) is generally translated as 'breath' or 'wind'.

In layman's terms, the Spirit of God is likened to a 'gust' or 'blast' of wind. Although wind is not visible, the evidence may be seen and felt whether in a whirlwind or gentle breeze. The Spirit of God was at work on 'the face of the waters' putting in order the particles that would form all living things. Some translators use the phrase 'brooding upon the face of the waters' as though the Spirit nurtured the earth as a hen broods over its young. The earth and sea at this time was the incubator to bring forth all life forms.

It is interesting that the Hebrew word for 'said' as in 'God said' is strikingly similar to the Hebrew word for 'vibration'. The mention first of light and the separation of light from the darkness and subsequent events that followed do have similarities with what science has put forward. Notice that although the sun was not created until the fourth day, evening and morning were the first day that embraced both day and night. The source of the mysterious light that was present before the sun, moon and stars is a mystery, however, whatever it was, it sustained the plants until the sun, moon, and stars appeared on the fourth day. Each separate species within the natural world consists of numbers whether based for example on the Golden Ratio, the Fibonacci sequence, or any other mathematical principle. If a single note from an instrument is flat or sharp in a symphony, the beauty of the music is lost. Even the untrained ear can recognize a single note out of tune. Without the spirit and Word, we would be void of imagination, vision, creativity, and void of any emotional connection to our feelings of love, gratitude, and praise. Even before we take our first breath of life, we sense things, and even if born physically blind, the divine reason does not prevent us from appreciating a symphony, a tasty meal, a touch of affection, a sweet aroma, or to 'see' with the imagination. The source of life does not come from flesh alone, just as knowledge does not come from mans' spirit alone. The spirit of Elohim enlightens the mind and gives us the ability to reason.

Day 2

1:6   And God said, Let there be a firmament in the midst of the waters, and let it divide the waters from the waters.

1:7	And God made the firmament, and divided the waters which were under the firmament from the waters which were above the firmament: and it was so.
1:8	And God called the firmament Heaven. And the evening and the morning were the second day.

Water and light are our most precious commodities. Here we observe the ingredients that sustain life on earth. Without water, atmosphere and light, there would be little chance of life. The earth first existed as a watery planet surrounded by a watery canopy above the earth and separated by an atmosphere.

Day 3

1:9	And God said, Let the waters under the heaven be gathered together unto one place, and let the dry land appear: and it was so.
1:10	And God called the dry land Earth; and the gathering together of the waters called the Seas: and God saw that it was good.

All the continents which we know of today were at this time one super continent that had eventually fragmented. Genesis 2 records that a 'mist' had watered the earth, evidently a mist generated from the four rivers that had flowed through the single land mass (Genesis 2:10-14). It is generally agreed this period was followed by the largest extinction of life in history. It was a time when survivors spread and re-colonised because of the splitting of the single land mass. Before the first rains had fallen, the earth had a watering system entirely different from what we have today. Genesis later speaks of a major disruption that had caused *the fountains of the depths* to be broken up simultaneously with the first rains that fell. Something of greater significance occurred to shift and split a single land mass to change the seasons. According to the record, the four seasons began because of a catastrophic change to the earth's surface that had occurred much later than this period (Genesis 7:11, 12. Genesis 8:2, 3).

1:11 And God said, Let the earth bring forth grass, the herb yielding seed, and the fruit tree yielding fruit after his kind, whose seed is in itself, upon the earth: and it was so.

1:12 And the earth brought forth grass, and herb yielding seed after his kind, and the tree yielding fruit, whose seed was in itself, after his kind: and God saw that it was good.

1:13 And the evening and the morning were the third day.

From the very beginning, plants, trees and herbs reproduced their own kind through the regeneration of 'the seed within itself'. Anything that is seed-bearing naturally dies and lives again. This principle applies to all living things. The Apostle Paul, when explaining life, death, and the regeneration of life wrote; *'What you sow is not made alive unless it dies'* (1 Corinthians 15:36-38). The cycle of life, death, and regeneration, was in play long before what was assumed to be a 'fall'. 'The seed within itself' is in the first chapter of Genesis because it holds a fundamental truth about the regeneration of life as it applies to all living things that eventually die (Genesis 1:11-12). If the evidence of the cycle of life and death through 'the seed within itself' is observable within the natural world of flora and fauna, is it unreasonable to think that the same principle applies to humanity?. The Apostle Paul explains:

> *But someone will say, "How are the dead raised up? And with what body do they come?" Foolish one, what you sow is not made alive unless it dies. And what you sow, you do not sow that body that shall be, but mere grain – perhaps wheat or some other grain. But God gives it a body as He pleases, and to each seed its own body* (1 Corinthians 45:35-41).

The natural world is a testimony to the regeneration of life regardless of everything deteriorating and eventually dying (1 Corinthians

15:35-42). Fire, flood, hurricanes, earthquakes, for example, may destroy what was once green valleys, mountains, plains, and human life, yet in a short time everything within the natural world is refreshed and replenished with new growth. Likewise, the human spirit finds the strength to carry on individually and collectively. Growing old and naturally dying should not be something to be feared, given what the Apostle Paul taught: 'to every seed his own body'. (1 Corinthians 15:38).

Each species has always held the blueprint that duplicates itself according to its own kind from one generation to the next. It is only within the seed that the deoxyribonucleic acid (DNA) string encodes the gene sequence of all who have existed before us. Through the gift of procreation, one or more of those hundreds of thousands of individual spermatozoa will eventually find its way to the ovum from where a new life begins. Medical science may observe the embryo forming physically in the womb, but no one can explain how or when spirit and flesh join within the womb.

> *Naked came I out of my mother's womb, and naked shall I return thither: the Lord gave, and the Lord hath taken away; blessed be the name of the Lord* (Job 1:21).

(The subject of the regeneration of life will be examined in the following chapter of Genesis)

Day 4

1:14   And God said, Let there be lights in the firmament of the heaven to divide the day from the night; and let them be for signs, and for seasons, and for days, and years:

1:15   And let them be for lights in the firmament of the heaven to give light upon the earth: and it was so.

1:16   And God made two great lights; the greater light to rule the day, and the lesser light to rule the night: he made the stars also.

1:17	And God set them in the firmament of the heaven to give light upon the earth,
1:18	And to rule over the day and over the night, and to divide the light from the darkness: and God saw that it was good.
1:19	And the evening and the morning were the fourth day.

Although the sun, moon and stars were not created until the fourth day, light was evident. This light was not a substitute for the sun, moon and stars, but what appears to be light from a separate source. By the fourth day, the sun, moon and stars illuminated the natural world so all living things could be replenished and reproduced. Throughout history mankind has relied on the movement and timing of the sun, moon, and stars, for the sowing and reaping of crops, navigation and reliance on the planetary bodies to influence the tides.

Day 5

1:20	And God said, Let the waters bring forth abundantly the moving creature that hath life, and fowl that may fly above the earth in the open firmament of heaven.
1:21	And God created great whales, and every living creature that moves, which the waters brought forth abundantly, after their kind, and every winged fowl after his kind: AND GOD SAW THAT IT WAS GOOD.
1:22	And God blessed them, saying, Be fruitful, and multiply, and fill the waters in the seas, and let fowl multiply in the earth.
1:23	And the evening and the morning were the fifth day.

The earth was once a single land mass surrounded by water and later subject to a global climatic change as described in Genesis 7:11,12.

If the days of creation extended to millions of years, it would have been on the fifth 'day' within the Mesozoic period that the dinosaurs appeared along with the 'great whales'. Dinosaurs were not necessarily restricted to land, since it appears the creatures that the 'waters brought forth abundantly' were amphibious and lived on the land and in the sea. Creationists should not assume that the larger, now extinct animals first appeared on the sixth day with the rest of the animals. Dinosaurs and all other large creatures of the sea, land, and sky that had appeared during the Triassic, Jurassic, and final Cretaceous period, marked the beginning and end of the Mesozoic era as described in Genesis chapter seven that finally saw a dramatic extinction and transition from larger to smaller animals.

For all that is known, the land under the water may have been fresh and consistently uniform and shallower than what we have today, perhaps turning salty because of the chemical change due to 'the fountains of the depths' that were broken up (Genesis 7:11, 12). Regardless of what took place, every variety of fish, birds, and animal life we find today, living or in fossil form, existed during this period. Although the earth and seas in which the creatures of the air depended were transformed during the Mesozoic stage, it wasn't until the splitting of the single land mass, coupled with a structural change to the earth that the climate could no longer sustain the giant birds and animals.

Day 6

1:24   And God said, Let the earth bring forth the living creature after his kind, cattle, and creeping thing, and beast of the earth after his kind: and it was so.

1:25   And God made the beast of the earth after his kind, and cattle after their kind, and everything that creepeth upon the earth after his kind: and God saw that it was good.

The closest companions to mankind are within the animal kingdom. The animals, insects, and creeping things that had appeared, were not to benefit man alone, but to maintain a balance within the natural world. The interaction between mankind, animals, and creeping things, is necessary for the survival of this planet. Although animals are endowed with intelligence and instincts for survival and capable of giving and receiving affection, they do not have the level of intellect and creativity that humans do.

1:26   And God said, Let us make man in our image, after our likeness: and let them have dominion over the fish of the sea, and over the fowl of the air, and over the cattle, and over all the earth, and over every creeping thing that creepeth upon the earth.

1:27   So God created man in his own image, in the image of God created he him; male and female created he them.

1:28   And God blessed them, and God said unto them, Be fruitful, and multiply, and replenish the earth, and subdue it: and have dominion over the fish of the sea, and over the fowl of the air, and over every living thing that moveth upon the earth.

Using the plural 'us' has been the subject of much debate for millennia. (This subject will be examined in Genesis 2). While those referred to here as 'male and female' were commanded to be 'fruitful, multiply, and replenish' the earth, the woman later formed from Adam's side had no idea about sex and procreation until she transgressed. Although the general rule when researching topics that require contextual evidence is based on the principle *'line upon line, precept upon precept, here a little, there a little'*, it appears this biblical rule is ignored when applied to the Genesis narrative (Isaiah 28:10). Although scripture explicitly states that incest is a sinful practice punishable by death, bible scholars nevertheless assume that Cain must have chosen a sister for a wife since there appears to be no other explanation. (Leviticus 18:18). The origin of Cain's wife will be examined in later chapters.

1:29   And God said, Behold, I have given you every herb bearing seed, which is upon the face of all the earth, and every tree, in the which is the fruit of a tree yielding seed; to you it shall be for meat.

Prehistoric man was naturally vegetarian with a life span between five hundred and nine hundred years (Genesis 5:1-32). Later we read of genealogies that record a remarkable list of ancestral names including the age when each patriarch had died. The longevity may have been due to a diet of fruit and herbs, although not proof that a vegan diet is necessarily the reason for such longevity. The soil may have been better balanced due to the chemical composition of the earth's crust. Genesis later shows it was not until the surface of the earth was transformed that the life span of mankind was reduced.

1:30   And to every beast of the earth, and to every fowl of the air, and to everything that creepeth upon the earth, wherein there is life, I have given every green herb for meat: and it was so.

According to the narrative, there was an abundance of 'green herbs' that sustained both man and beast while supporting a closer connection between them. We have many predatory species today but not because of an original sin. It was only after the single land mass had gone through a dramatic change that food became scarce, a scarcity that may well have been the trigger for predatory behaviour. Although the earth went through a change that altered the seasons as described in Genesis 8:22, 'the seed within itself', already dormant within the earth and under the water, reproduced life. Wherever the elements and climate were right for a particular seed to germinate and flourish, life on earth was renewed.

> **1:31** And God saw everything that he had made, and, behold, it was very good. And the evening and the morning were the sixth day.

The natural wonders within the sea, earth, and sky are testimony to how the earth is replenished and cared for by the interaction between all living things. By now every living thing in nature could reproduce life after its own kind. Every variety within each separate species has a set incubation period that determines a time to be born, followed by a fixed cycle of time that determines the lifespan.

Genesis Chapter 2

Day 7

2:1	Thus the heavens and the earth were finished, and all the host of them
2:2	And on the seventh day God ended his work which he had made; and he rested on the seventh day from all his work which he had made.

Whether one believes that the period between the first and the sixth day extended for millennia to enable the separate species to develop within their limits of adaptation, or whether one believes this period was a cycle of six, twenty-four hour periods, the narrative is clear that the works of creation were completed by the sixth day with the seventh day reserved for a perpetual rest. Given that the first day had begun with the creation of light and then the separation of the darkness from the light, followed by the separation of earth and sky with an atmosphere, and then the emergence of land from out of the water before any living thing appeared, speaks volumes of just how much the ancients must have known about the cosmos and laws of physics. It is interesting that whilst science is of the view that life began in the sea and progressed from there, Genesis is also clear that the first forms of life, besides the plants, were fish, then birds, then the animals, then finally mankind, in that order.

2:2	And on the seventh day God ended his work which he had made; and he rested on the seventh day from all his work which he had made.
2:3	And God blessed the seventh day, and sanctified it: because that in it he had rested from all his work which God created and made.

Genesis presents a separate account of the seventh day because the seventh day does not conclude with an 'evening and morning'. To say that God blessed and set aside one day as holy during this period of time is to deny the sacredness of every other day. All time is holy and blessed. We later learn that the failure of Israel to trust and live by faith was the cause of their losing sight of the meaning about the 'day' that was a permanent 'spiritual rest'. It was necessary to change the spiritual rest to a physical rest many millennia later because the 'true rest' had lost its meaning. The seventh day had no need for an 'evening and morning' as the 'day' was a perpetual day and perpetual spiritual rest.

Some would argue that a seventh day 'evening to evening' was kept by the descendants of Adam and Seth and through to Abraham and his descendants, but this argument is not in keeping with the true meaning of the limitless boundary of time that had no need for an evening and morning (Hebrews 4:3-11).

2:4	These are the generations of the heavens and of the earth when they were created, in the day that the Lord God made the earth and the heavens,

The New Testament refers to the period of Jesus' ministry and the age of the gospel as the 'day of the Lord', a period that extended further than a twenty-four hour day. What does Isaiah mean when he asks *'shall the earth be made to give birth in one day, or shall a nation be born at once?'* (Isaiah 66:8). Some scholars suggest that when the Hebrew word Yom (day) is preceded by the definite article (as in first Yom, second Yom and so on), Yom refers to a 24-hour cycle. Other scholars disagree, since each day may have represented a thousand years, or seven thousand years, while others argue that the 'day' here refers to millions or perhaps billions of years. Genesis chapter one describes the days of creation with an evening and morning as the first day, second day, and so on, while Genesis chapter two refers to the separate days of creation as 'generations'. The whole time structure is referred to in this chapter as 'the day when the Lord God made the earth and the heavens'.

In the previous few verses the Hebrew word Elohim אֱלֹהִים denotes duality while the Hebrew word Yahweh יְהוָה places the word 'Lord' before 'God' in recognition of the creative power of the one Lord God as the figurative 'Father and Son' within the Elohim. Here we see the finished work of creation and the beginning of the interaction between the figurative Father and Son within the logos.

2:5 And every plant of the field before it was in the earth, and every herb of the field before it grew: for the Lord God had not caused it to rain upon the earth, and there was not a man to till the ground.

2:6 But there went up a mist from the earth, and watered the whole face of the ground.

2:7 And the Lord God formed man of the dust of the ground, and breathed into his nostrils the breath of life; and man became a living soul.

2:8 And the Lord God planted a garden eastward in Eden; and there he put the man whom he had formed.

2:9 And out of the ground made the Lord God to grow every tree that is pleasant to the sight, and good for food; the tree of life also in the garden, and the tree of knowledge of good and evil.

Before the 'man' was formed and 'put' in a garden separate from the earth, our attention is first drawn to 'the third day' when the plants, herbs, and fruit trees had appeared. Obviously somebody had to dress and keep the garden, including the tree of life and the tree of knowledge of good and evil that had appeared on day three. As already observed from Genesis chapter one, while the plants, herbs, and trees appeared on day three, the sun, moon and stars hadn't appeared until day four, therefore the elements were not in order for the rains to fall. Here we observe the day when Adam was 'put' in a separate place from the earth and the reason he was formed before the sun, moon, and stars. Adam was formed on the third day and was with the Father before the sun, moon, and stars and before there was life in the sea, birds of the air or before all the animals and insects had appeared. The Son of God was there when it was said *'let us make man in our image, after our likeness'* (Genesis 1:26). Adam was *the firstborn of every creature* and *the beginning of the creation of God* within humanity. He was *before all things, and in whom all things consist* (Colossians 1:15-19. Revelation 3:14. John 1:1-5. 1:14.).

> *Who is the image of the invisible God, the firstborn of every creature: For by him were all things created, that are in heaven, and that are in earth, visible and invisible, whether they be thrones, or dominions, or principalities, or powers: all things were created by him, and for him: And he is before all things, and by him all things consist. And he is the head of the body, the church: who is the beginning, the firstborn from the dead; that in all things he might have the preeminence. For it pleased the Father that in him should all fulness dwell* (Colossians 1:15-19);

Before the foundation of the world, the pre-existing Word would appear again in an earthly body through the seed of procreation and through the blood of Adam's descendants.

> *For unto which of the angels said he at any time, Thou art my Son, this day have I begotten thee? And again, I will be to him a Father, and he shall be to me a Son? And again, when he bringeth in the firstbegotten into the world, he saith, And let all the angels of God worship him* (Hebrews 1:5, 6).

The word 'again' refers to the first natural man whom appeared a second time as the 'last Adam'. The interaction between the Father and Son drew to a close the night before the crucifixion when Jesus had uttered his final prayer. His words on Calvary's cross; 'It is finished', reflect what he had said the night before his crucifixion *'I have finished the work which thou gavest me to do'*.

> *Father, the hour is come; glorify thy Son, that thy Son also may glorify thee: As thou hast given him power over all flesh, that he should give eternal life to as many as thou hast given him. And this is life eternal, that they might know thee the only true God, and Jesus Christ, whom thou hast sent. I have glorified thee on the earth: I have finished the work which thou gavest me to do. And now, O Father, glorify thou me with thine own self with the glory which I had with thee before the world was* (John 17:1b-5).

2:10   And a river went out of Eden to water the garden; and from thence it was parted, and became into four heads.

2:11   The name of the first is Pison: that is it which compasseth the whole land of Havilah, where there is gold;

2:12   And the gold of that land is good: there is bdellium and the onyx stone.

2:13   And the name of the second river is Gihon: the same is it that compasseth the whole land of Ethiopia.

2:14   And the name of the third river is Hiddekel: that is it which goeth toward the east of Assyria. And the fourth river is Euphrates.

2:15   And the Lord God took the man, and put him into the Garden of Eden to dress it and to keep it.

It is interesting that the four rivers are mentioned immediately after Adam was formed. Yet although those who inhabited the earth were not created until the sixth day, a 'mist' had watered the earth while the garden was managed by Adam who most likely had channelled water from the river that flowed through the garden. The four separate rivers mentioned here had not only provided the mist that watered the single land mass but also represent the geographical areas later to be inhabited by four separate races that occupied the banks of the rivers that flowed from Eden. Although the evidence of four original races occupying the banks of the four rivers may be circumstantial, the following commentary on Revelation chapter six reveals a striking similarity with the four separate coloured horses that take the gospel to the four corners of the earth.

2:16   And the Lord God commanded the man, saying, Of every tree of the garden thou mayest freely eat:

2:17   But of the tree of the knowledge of good and evil, thou shalt not eat of it: for in the day that thou eatest thereof thou shalt surely die.

Following the description of the four rivers, our attention is immediately drawn back to Adam's role in the garden. Here we observe that Adam is aware of the tree of knowledge of good and evil and consequences of partaking from the tree before Eve was formed.

2:18   And the Lord God said, It is not good that the man should be alone; I will make him an help meet for him.

2:19   And out of the ground the Lord God formed every beast of the field, and every fowl of the air; and brought them unto Adam to see what he would call them: and whatsoever Adam called every living creature, that was the name thereof.

2:20   And Adam gave names to all cattle, and to the fowl of the air, and to every beast of the field; but for Adam there was not found an help meet for him.

2:21	And the Lord God caused a deep sleep to fall upon Adam, and he slept: and he took one of his ribs, and closed up the flesh instead thereof;
2:22	And the rib, which the Lord God had taken from man, made he a woman, and brought her unto the man.
2:23	And Adam said, This is now bone of my bones, and flesh of my flesh: she shall be called Woman, because she was taken out of Man.
2:24	Therefore shall a man leave his father and his mother, and shall cleave unto his wife: and they shall be one flesh.
2:25	And they were both naked, the man and his wife, and were not ashamed.

It is hard to imagine how Adam would have had time within a literal twenty four hour day to name every land animal and amphibious creature on the same day he was put in a deep sleep. It is more likely that Adam named the amphibians and land animals on the same day each creature had appeared. Here we notice that Adam also named the 'fowls of the air' that appeared on the fifth day. The only possibility in explaining how the 'man' could survive for eons of time through the Mesozoic era, is that the man, later named Adam, existed in another dimension of time and in a different form, albeit 'a living being' with an earthly body that later went through two transitional changes. Genesis records that Adam was put in a 'deep sleep' only after he had named all the living creatures.

From Adam's deep sleep, a female was formed in the image of Adam since there was nothing amongst the animal kingdom comparable to him. This was the first transitional change necessary so his female companion could bear the seed to accomplish all that was before him.

Here we notice that Eve was not ashamed of her nakedness because she had not yet reached out and tasted from the tree of the knowledge of good and evil. The context of a single woman and single man shows the distinction between those created out on the earth compared to the woman who had no idea about sexual desire and procreation until she transgressed.

There is no certainty as to what length of time the six days of creation extended to. It's unlikely that 'evening and morning' was the same time period that exists today. Where did evening start, and where did morning end during this era? Evening today could be any time from noon to early night, while morning could be any time after midnight until noon. The evening and morning may indicate a different cycle of time during this era. Genesis later speaks of the earth going through a significant change in both structure and what was possibly a re-positioning of the axis that caused such violence to the earth (Genesis 7:11,12). Something had interrupted both the topography of the single land mass and had altered time as we know it today.

THE GENESIS CHRONOLOGY

The following Genesis chronology is a re-sequencing of all the verses from Genesis 1 and 2 that shows the distinction between the forming of Adam separate from those out on the earth. It is worth noting that not one verse from Genesis 1 and 2 has been omitted. One may ask: why then wasn't the narrative written plainly in the first place? It is the author's considered opinion that a parallel message was deliberately hidden to protect the knowledge of the seed that was to bring the Christ child into the world. That Herod requested the death of the Christ child is testimony to why the seed that was to bring life and immortality to light through the gospels, had to be hidden through the ages (Colossians 1:26).

Day 1.

In the beginning God created the heaven and the earth. And the earth was without form, and void; and darkness was upon the face of the deep. And the Spirit of God moved upon the face of the waters. And God said, Let there be light: and there was light. And God saw the light, that it was good: and God divided the light from the darkness. And God called the light Day, and the darkness he called Night. And the evening and the morning were the first day.

Day 2.

And God said, Let there be a firmament in the midst of the waters, and let it divide the waters from the waters. And God made the firmament, and divided the waters which were under the firmament from the waters which were above the firmament: and it was so. And God called the firmament Heaven. And the evening and the morning were the second day.

Day 3.

And God said, Let the waters under the heaven be gathered together unto one place, and let the dry land appear: and it was so. And God called the dry land Earth; and the gathering together of the waters called he Seas: and God saw that it was good. And God said, Let the earth bring forth grass, the herb yielding seed, and the fruit tree yielding fruit after his kind, whose seed is in itself, upon the earth: and it was so. And the earth brought forth grass, and herb yielding seed after his kind, and the tree yielding fruit, whose seed was in itself, after his kind: and God saw that it was good. And every plant of the field before it was in the earth, and every herb of the field before it grew: for the Lord God had not caused it to rain upon the earth, and there was not a man to till the ground. But there went up a mist from the earth, and watered the whole face of the ground. And the Lord God formed man of the dust of the ground, and breathed into his nostrils the breath of life; and man became a living soul. And the Lord God planted a garden eastward in Eden; and there he put the man whom he had formed.And a river went out of Eden to water the garden; and from thence it was parted, and became into four heads. The name of the first is Pison: that is it which compasseth the whole land of Havilah, where there is gold; And the gold of that land is good: there is bdellium and the onyx stone. And the name of the second river is Gihon: the same is it that compasseth the whole land of Ethiopia. And the name of the third river is Hiddekel: that is it which goeth toward the east of Assyria. And the fourth river is Euphrates. And out of the ground made the Lord God to grow every tree that is pleasant to the sight, and good for food; the tree of life also in the midst of the garden, and the tree of knowledge of good and evil. And the Lord God took the man, and put him into the Garden of Eden to dress it and to keep it. And the Lord God commanded the man, saying, Of every tree of the garden thou mayest freely eat: But of the tree of the knowledge of good and evil, thou shalt not eat of it: for in the day that thou eatest thereof thou shalt surely die. And the evening and the morning were the third day.

Day 4.

And God said, Let there be lights in the firmament of the heaven to divide the day from the night; and let them be for signs, and for seasons, and for days, and years: And let them be for lights in the firmament of the heaven to give light upon the earth: and it was so. And God made two great lights; the greater light to rule the day, and the lesser light to rule the night: he made the stars also. And God set them in the firmament of the heaven to give light upon the earth, and to rule over the day and over the night, and to divide the light from the darkness: and God saw that it was good. And the evening and the morning were the fourth day.

Day 5.

And God said, Let the waters bring forth abundantly the moving creature that hath life, and fowl that may fly above the earth in the open firmament of heaven. And God created great whales, and every living creature that moveth, which the waters brought forth abundantly, after their kind, and every winged fowl after his kind: and God saw that it was good. And God blessed them, saying, Be fruitful, and multiply, and fill the waters in the seas, and let fowl multiply in the earth. And the evening and the morning were the fifth day.

Day 6.

And God said, Let the earth bring forth the living creature after his kind, cattle, and creeping thing, and beast of the earth after his kind: and it was so. And God made the beast of the earth after his kind, and cattle after their kind, and every thing that creepeth upon the earth after his kind: and God saw that it was good. And out of the ground the Lord God formed every beast of the field, and every fowl of the air; and brought them unto Adam to see what he would call them: and whatsoever Adam called every living creature, that was the name thereof. And Adam gave names to all cattle, and to the fowl of the air, and to every beast of the field; but for Adam there was not found an help meet for him. And God said, Let us make mankind in our image, after our likeness: and let them have dominion over the fish of the sea, and over the fowl of the air, and over the cattle, and over all the earth, and over every creeping thing that creepeth upon the earth. So God created mankind in his own image, in the image of God created he him; male and female created he them. And God blessed them, and God said unto them, Be fruitful, and multiply, and replenish the earth, and subdue it: and have dominion over the fish of the sea, and over the fowl of the air, and over every living thing that moveth upon the earth. And God said, Behold, I have given you every herb bearing seed, which is upon the face of all the earth, and every tree, in the which is the fruit of a tree yielding seed; to you it shall be for meat. And to every beast of the earth, and to every fowl of the air, and to every thing that creepeth upon the earth, wherein there is life, I have given every green herb for meat: and it was so. And the Lord God said, It is not good that the man should be alone; I will make him an help meet for him. And the Lord God caused a deep sleep to fall upon Adam, and he slept: and he took one of his ribs, and closed up the flesh instead thereof; And the rib, which the Lord God had taken from man, made he a woman, and brought her unto the man. And Adam said, This is now bone of my bones, and flesh of my flesh: she shall be called Woman, because she was taken out of Man. Therefore shall a man leave his father and his mother, and shall cleave unto his wife: and they shall be one flesh. And they were both naked, the man and his wife, and were not ashamed. And God saw every thing that he had made, and, behold, it was very good. And the evening and the morning were the sixth day.*

Day 7.

Thus the heavens and the earth were finished, and all the host of them. And on the seventh day God ended his work which he had made; and he rested on the seventh day from all his work which he had made. And God blessed the seventh day, and sanctified it: because that in it he had rested from all his work which God created and made. These are the generations of the heavens and of the earth when they were created, in the day that the Lord God made the earth and the heavens. (Genesis 1: 1-31, Genesis 2: 1-25).

Genesis Chapter 3

3:1 Now the serpent was more subtil than any beast of the field which the Lord God had made. And he said unto the woman, Yea, hath God said, Ye shall not eat of every tree of the garden?

3:2 And the woman said unto the serpent, We may eat of the fruit of the trees of the garden:

3:3 But of the fruit of the tree which is in the midst of the garden, God hath said, Ye shall not eat of it, neither shall ye touch it, lest ye die.

3:4 And the serpent said unto the woman, Ye shall not surely die:

3:5 For God doth know that in the day ye eat thereof, then your eyes shall be opened, and ye shall be as gods, knowing good and evil.

3:6 And when the woman saw that the tree was good for food, and that it was pleasant to the eyes, and a tree to be desired to make one wise, she took of the fruit thereof, and did eat, and gave also unto her husband with her; and he did eat.

3:7 And the eyes of them both were opened, and they knew that they were naked; and they sewed fig leaves together, and made themselves aprons.

Contrary to tradition, Eden was never intended to be the place where copulation was to begin, neither a place where offspring would forever be bound by law. The most fundamental teaching from the New Testament is the subject of law and grace. The Apostle Paul cautioned why such rules as *'do not handle, do not touch, do not taste'* are contrary to all who are Christ minded, therefore the congregation was advised to refrain from such teachings.

> *Since you died with Christ to the elemental spiritual forces of this world, why, as though you still belonged to the world, do you submit to its rules: "Do not handle! Do not taste! Do not touch!"? These rules, which have to do with things that are all destined to perish with use, are based on merely human commands and teachings. Such regulations indeed have an appearance of wisdom, with their self-imposed worship, their false humility and their harsh treatment of the body, but they lack any value in restraining sensual indulgence* (Colossians 2:20-23. NIV)

Paul's statement reinforces just why *'Christ is the end of the law for righteousness'* and why the command *'do not taste, do not touch'* had to be ignored should Eve decide to have her eyes opened to the knowledge of good and evil. Without the knowledge of good and evil, the fruits of the spirit; *'love, joy, peace, patience, kindness, goodness, faithfulness, gentleness and self-control'*, would be meaningless. Those fruits reflect the image and likeness of God. Concerning the fruits of the spirit, the Apostle Paul could confidently say: *against such things there is no law'* (Galatians 5: 22, 23).

The serpent's message *'ye shall be as gods knowing good and evil'* is not exclusive to Eve alone, but to all. Consider Jesus' words

> *"Is it not written in your law, 'I said, "You are gods"'? If He called them gods, to whom the Word of God came (and the Scripture cannot be broken), do you say of Him whom the Father sanctified and sent into the world, 'You are blaspheming,' because I said, 'I am the Son of God'?* (John 10: 34 - 36).

There are three explicit truths here that cannot be ignored. First, Eve's eyes were opened to good and evil and therefore had become like God only because of her transgression. Second, Eve was aware of her nakedness and ability to procreate only because of a transgression. Third, although Eve's physical body had begun to die because of a transgression, the spirit within her perishable body remained everlasting through regeneration and procreation of the flesh. To suggest that the serpent's lie had initiated a rescue plan to save sinners because of a 'fall' contradicts everything Genesis teaches about Eve's choice to have her nakedness revealed, have offspring, grow old, and eventually die naturally.

Genesis teaches a fundamental lesson about the distinction between Adam, Eve, and 'mankind', and the reason for that dissimilarity. For example, Eve was in a 'garden' and separate from the 'earth' and had no idea about sex and procreation until she partook from the tree of knowledge. There was only one living being *'more subtil than any beast of the field'* that could open Eve's eyes to the blessings of procreation. However, she must first let go of the security of the garden and accept that having the knowledge of good and evil would have consequences.

Only Adam, the Son of God, had the subtlety and reasoning power to persuade Eve to step out of her innocence. It was necessary for Adam to reason with Eve about the blessings of procreation despite the consequences of having the knowledge of good and evil. Adam symbolically spoke as a 'serpent' because Eve had to inderstand the consequences of sin. Adam had persuaded Eve that even with her choosing a limited life span, she would not die in vain. Eve saw it was the knowledge of good and evil that held the key to procreation, regardless of what would happen outside of Eden. She realised that everlasting life without offspring, could only offer a selfish existence. Eve partook of the fruit knowing that her eyes would be opened to the blessing of love and procreation and knew despite the consequences of evil, her offspring would bear the fruit that would bring life and immortality to light through the gospels (2 Timothy 1:10). The Apostle Paul speaks about Eve's submission to the serpent, not as one who committed a sin, but one persuaded by the voice of reason.

But I fear, lest by any means, as the serpent beguiled Eve through his subtlety, so your minds should be corrupted from the simplicity that is in Christ (2 Corinthians 11:3).

Although Paul speaks about Eve being deceived by craftiness, he is not saying that what took place between herself and the serpent was an act of rebellion. Eve had to think for herself about life outside the boundaries of the garden. Paul is not saying that Eve's mind was corrupted by a serpent, but bringing home a lesson as to how one may be persuaded or may persuade others through the power of reasoning with intent whether for good or evil. Eve could have remained ignorant of her nakedness and without the desire to procreate, but she purposely had her eyes opened once she realised what life outside the garden would bring.

Both Jesus and Moses had pointed to the symbolic serpent, not as the cause of sin, but as the remedy for sin. Notice Jesus' statement:

And the Lord said unto Moses, Make thee a fiery serpent, and set it upon a pole: and it shall come to pass, that every one that is bitten, when he looketh upon it, shall live. (Numbers 27:8)

The most effective remedy for a serpent's venom is found within the serpent itself. When the *last* Adam, Jesus, was elevated on a pole, he had willingly become the figurative serpent that held the remedy for those who would fall victim to sin because of the knowledge of good and evil. It could only be the Son of God who could bring humanity together as one, therefore no one aside from Adam could do the Father's will.

Before Jesus was crucified, he had reiterated what Moses had said;

And as Moses lifted up the serpent in the wilderness, even so must the Son of man be lifted up: That whosoever believeth in him should not perish, but have eternal life (John 3: 14,15).

The *first* Adam opened the door to the knowledge of good and evil and the *last* Adam held the remedy for all infected with the venom of sin. What other symbol but a 'serpent' would be more fitting for the one who had no option but to introduce humanity to the knowledge of good and evil for the sake of 'becoming like God'? (Genesis 3:22). The one who had opened the door that no man could shut was also the one who finally shut the door on all infected with the venom of sin (Revelation 3:7, 8).

3:8   And they heard the voice of the Lord God walking in the garden in the cool of the day: and Adam and his wife hid themselves from the presence of the Lord God amongst the trees of the garden.

3:9   And the Lord God called unto Adam, and said unto him, Where art thou?

3:10 And he said, I heard thy voice in the garden, and I was afraid, because I was naked; and I hid myself.

3:11 And he said, Who told thee that thou wast naked? Hast thou eaten of the tree, whereof I commanded thee that thou shouldest not eat?

3:12 And the man said, The woman whom thou gavest to be with me, she gave me of the tree, and I did eat.

3:13 And the Lord God said unto the woman, What is this that thou hast done? And the woman said, The serpent beguiled me, and I did eat.

3:14 And the Lord God said unto the serpent, Because thou hast done this, thou art cursed above all cattle, and above every beast of the field; upon thy belly shalt thou go, and dust shalt thou eat all the days of thy life:

3:15 And I will put enmity between thee and the woman, and between thy seed and her seed; it shall bruise thy head, and thou shalt bruise his heel.

According to the scriptures, God is spirit, not flesh and blood (John 4:24). The following communication between the Lord God, Adam, Eve, and the Serpent, does not necessarily mean that the Lord God

(Yahweh Elohim) is audibly speaking (John 4:24). Here we see once again the interaction between the figurative Father and Son to vindicate the Father. The voice of Yahweh Elohim denotes the awareness between a Father and Son interacting within the spirit and logos of Elohim. Adam as a firstborn son is here in the flesh beside Eve and consciously aware that he must take full responsibility for Eve's decision to transgress for the sake of her becoming like God in image and likeness. It is the 'Father' within the Elohim that wills the Son to lay bare the consequences of knowing of good and evil. Because the 'alpha of God' willingly bid the Father's will, here we observe that Adam is taking full responsibility by accepting all that is about to be said by the Father.

Although Eve first transgressed, it is Adam whom the Father first addresses. Adam is 'afraid' only because he is naked in the presence of the Father. He neither blames the Father, Eve, or the serpent, but simply states that what Eve had partaken of, he also willingly accepted. Likewise, Eve simply states she was 'beguiled' by the serpent, and admits that it was her choice. The curse addressed to the symbolic serpent is a message to all who would follow the path of evil. The potential to sin is within each of us since becoming like God, therefore being on one's belly and eating the dust expresses just how low individuals and humanity can go since partaking from the tree of knowledge. From the head we conceive sin, and with the heel we may crush evil before it strikes. For example, while Abraham's twin sons Esau and Jacob were in their mother's womb, the enmity between them was already evident. Jacob was later named Israel while Esau was the father of the Edomites, a nation that later plagued Israel (Genesis 35:10, Obadiah 1:1-21). The twin brothers' destinies were already sealed from within the womb (Genesis 25:22-24). Although, according to the Apostle Paul, 'many' were to inevitably choose the path of evil, so too, 'many' would choose the path of righteousness (Romans 5:10).

Adam knew he was in a sanctified and holy place and mindful that the garden was a restricted area where copulating was prohibited. He knew his nakedness would be revealed once again in the presence of the Father and humanity on Calvary's hill. The humiliation that the last Adam endured can only be understood in context of the day when the Son of God echoed David's cry;

> *'My God, My God, why have you forsaken me?'* (Psalm 22:1, Matthew 27:46).

The first Adam willingly departed the garden because he was the only one who could abolish the enmity between the flesh and the spirit that potentially separated God and humanity. God is spirit and man is flesh, therefore the enmity between the flesh and spirit was finally reconciled when the *last* Adam, Jesus, created one new man in Christ (Ephesians 2:14-19). There is no excuse for the enmity that exists to this day between the descendants of Abraham's two sons - Isaac and Ishmael, the fathers of the Jews and Arabs.

> *For he is our peace, who hath made both one, and hath broken down the middle wall of partition between us; Having abolished in his flesh the enmity, even the law of commandments contained in ordinances; for to make in himself of twain one new man, so making peace; And that he might reconcile both unto God in one body by the cross, having slain the enmity thereby: And came and preached peace to you which were afar off, and to them that were nigh. For through him we both have access by one Spirit unto the Father. Now therefore ye are no more strangers and foreigners, but fellow citizens with the saints, and of the household of God; And are built upon the foundation of the Apostles and prophets, Jesus Christ himself being the chief corner stone; In whom all the building fitly framed together groweth unto an holy temple in the Lord: In whom ye also are builded together for an habitation of God through the Spirit* (Ephesians 2:14-22).

From the Garden of Eden, Adam willingly surrendered the glory he had with the Father, and from the Garden of Gethsemane the last Adam, Jesus, uttered the words:

> *I have glorified thee on the earth: I have finished the work which thou gavest me to do. And now, O Father, glorify thou me with thine own self with the glory which I had with thee before the world was* (John 17: 4,5).

3:16   Unto the woman he said, I will greatly multiply thy sorrow and thy conception; in sorrow thou shalt bring forth children; and thy desire shall be to thy husband, and he shall rule over thee.

If Eve had the desire to procreate since being formed from Adam's side, the dialogue between herself and the 'serpent' would not have been necessary. Her sorrow multiplied, not because the earth changed its nature, but because she would have offspring out in the earth and live and die naturally like the rest of mankind. Although Eve knew many of her offspring would choose the path of evil, she was mindful that through her offspring, redemption would be offered.

3:17   And unto Adam he said, Because thou hast hearkened unto the voice of thy wife, and hast eaten of the tree, of which I commanded thee, saying, Thou shalt not eat of it: cursed is the ground for thy sake; in sorrow shalt thou eat of it all the days of thy life;

3:18   Thorns also and thistles shall it bring forth to thee; and thou shalt eat the herb of the field;

The Father cannot be blamed for introducing Adam and Eve's offspring to the knowledge of good and evil. Here we see no argument or blame from Adam but acknowledgment of his willingness to do the Father's will. Contrary to tradition, Adam was not cursed, but the ground itself was cursed for the generations that followed. Adam and Eve were aware that although there was to be toil amongst the thorns and thistles, there were also blessings to follow. Our forefathers' struggles in bringing knowledge and understanding to us were not without blood, sweat, and tears. The races occupying the rivers out in the earth were already toiling and enjoying edible herbs as already noted from Genesis chapter one.

'Behold I have given you every herb bearing seed which is upon the face of all the earth, and every tree in which is the fruit of a tree yielding seed, to you it shall be for meat' (Genesis 1:26-31).

3:19 In the sweat of thy face shalt thou eat bread, till thou return unto the ground; for out of it wast thou taken: for dust thou art, and unto dust shalt thou return.

Living in a garden utopia for eternity without the knowledge of good and evil would be meaningless. Life would not be as fulfilling had the couple in the garden not had the opportunity to be creative and productive while using the resources that the natural world provides.

3:20 And Adam called his wife's name Eve; because she was the mother of all living.

Through Eve, the promised seed was to bring the fullness of Christ into the world; therefore not one amongst mankind besides Eve could claim to be 'the mother of all living'. Bringing new life into the world is often remembered as an experience of joy and celebration rather than remembered for the pain associated with childbearing. Love and procreation is the guarantee of everlasting life in Christ, therefore Eve is mentioned here as 'the mother of all living'.

3:21 Unto Adam also and to his wife did the Lord God make coats of skins, and clothed them.

Before Adam and Eve had gone out into the earth, they were clothed with 'coats of skins'. The Hebrew word for skin עור does not necessarily depict the skin of an animal as a covering, but the actual skin of Adam and Eve. The same Hebrew word for skin is found again in Exodus 34:30, 35 as in *'behold, the skin of his face'*, or *'the skin of Moses'*. Whatever was the physical appearance of Adam since being formed a 'living being' along with Eve later formed from Adam, a different type of protective skin was now needed due to the changed environment they were about to enter. This was Adam's second transitional change and Eve's first transitional change. The record states that Adam was nine hundred and thirty five years of age when he died, which may indicate that only since he exited Eden his days were numbered (Genesis 5:5) .

> 3:22 And the Lord God said, Behold, the man is become as one of us, to know good and evil: and now, lest he put forth his hand, and take also of the tree of life, and eat, and live for ever:

That the 'man' had 'become as one of us' holds a profound lesson about the nature of Adam and his descendants. Here we see the difference between mankind already occupying the earth, and Adam's offspring. Those beyond the boundaries of Eden, although created in the image and likeness of God and commanded to immediately multiply and replenish the earth, were without hope of redemption. It was only through the promised seed preserved within the blood of Adam's descendants that those formed separately from Adam could be redeemed. The figurative Father and Son are here speaking about the entire race of humanity called 'man'.

The *last* Adam was *born of the seed of David, according to the flesh* (Romans 1:3, 4). As the Apostle Paul affirms, when the last Adam appeared again he was the exact image and imprint of the original firstborn of creation. As previously noted, the original Greek word for 'type' (τύπος) does not simply represent a copy of the original, but the exact imprint of the original (Romans 5:14).

> 3:23 Therefore the Lord God sent him forth from the Garden of Eden, to till the ground from whence he was taken.

3:24	So he drove out the man; and he placed at the east of the Garden of Eden Cherubims, and a flaming sword which turned every way, to keep the way of the tree of life.

The knowledge of our beginnings was to be guarded lest we lose sight of the true meaning of 'the tree of life' as it relates to procreation and the regeneration of life. It was necessary to place figurative cherubs to preserve 'the way of the tree of life' since copulation was forbidden within a holy place. The figurative cherubim were not commanded to guard the tree of life itself, but 'to keep the way' of the tree of life. The 'tree of life' is humanity's guarantee of everlasting life through each family tree. 'The tree of life' and 'the tree of knowledge' hold one truth, and that truth is the inseparable link between everlasting spiritual life, and temporary life in the flesh. There would be no meaning to life without the knowledge of good and evil, therefore Eve had to choose whether to live forever without offspring or whether to partake of the knowledge of good and evil and accept that life, death, and regeneration through procreation would ensure everlasting life of body, mind, and spirit through the figurative 'tree of life'.

Genesis Chapter 4

4:1   And Adam knew Eve his wife; and she conceived, and bare Cain, and said, I have gotten a man from the Lord.

4:2   And she again bare his brother Abel. And Abel was a keeper of sheep, but Cain was a tiller of the ground.

Adam is mentioned here as 'Lord' since Eve had acknowledged his position in the family as husband and father of her offspring and also as Lord of all who were to call on 'the name of the Lord' (Genesis 4:26). Using the word 'again' may indicate that Cain and Abel were twins. The first-born twin serving the second born is not unusual as was the case of Esau and Jacob.

Abel was 'a keeper of sheep', while Cain was 'a tiller of the ground'. This may appear to indicate a less important calling for Cain, but no one is less important than another. Although everyone enters life with gifts and talents, many fail to recognise their gifts for various reasons. While we cannot be everything to everyone, there is something unique about each of us. One may be born to sing, another an athlete, inventor, and so on. As we grow from child to adult we recognise that we each have unique gifts and talents as was the case of Cain and Abel.

4:3   And in process of time it came to pass, that Cain brought of the fruit of the ground an offering unto the Lord.

> **4:4** And Abel, he also brought of the firstlings of his flock and of the fat thereof. And the Lord had respect unto Abel and to his offering:

Genesis is here reiterating the importance of Adam's role as Lord. He is both Lord and husband of a family. Once again, the term Lord instead of Adam cannot be overlooked. By now the brothers had grown to a mature age where their appreciation for their Lord and father was shown by presenting gifts and offerings. There is no mention of the ages of Cain and Abel other than 'in the process of time' and 'it came to pass', which could mean any number of years. The term 'process of time' is used by many creationists as evidence that Adam and Eve bore many other children while Cain and Abel were growing into adults. To contend that Adam and Eve had ample time to bear more children for Cain to select a sister for a wife contradicts the explicit teaching that brother and sister are strictly forbidden to have a sexual relationship (Leviticus 18:9,29,30).

Cain's offering of the fruit of the ground was the offering of his own toiling while Abel's offering was the product that grew from the goodness and richness the earth had provided with no effort. Notice that Abel's offering was 'the firstlings and the fat of his flock', not the actual fat gathered by slaughtering an animal. Abel simply offered healthy lambs or 'firstlings' of his flock as a result of Cain's toiling. At this stage Cain had not yet murdered his brother, yet it is assumed this offering was the first blood offering that typified atonement for sin. Cain believed his works to be of more praise than Abel's offering seeing that Abel had done nothing that had contributed to the fattening of his animals.

> **4:5** But unto Cain and to his offering he had not respect. And Cain was very wroth, and his countenance fell.
>
> **4:6** And the Lord said unto Cain, Why art thou wroth? and why is thy countenance fallen?

4:7	If thou doest well, shalt thou not be accepted? and if thou doest not well, sin lieth at the door. And unto thee shall be his desire, and thou shalt rule over him.

It was unfair, at least to Cain, that Adam had more respect for Abel's offering when there was no toil involved on Abel's part. However, Abel had acknowledged by his gift that without the goodness of the earth there would be nothing to offer. Cain overlooked a vital lesson; he failed to see that being his brother's keeper would have been his greatest offering. To this day the question *'am I my brother's keeper?'* is still ignored by many. We each have the power to 'rule over sin' rather than allowing sin's power to rule over us. There may be a reason for jealousy and anger, but there is no excuse for murder.

In the story of Cain and Abel we learn of the first instance of one who chose evil over good. Rather than controlling what was about to overpower him, Cain was preparing himself for an argument. This was the first account of ignoring the law written on the heart. Cain was aware of his potential to be evil therefore he was described by Jesus as *'the devil from the beginning'*. Cain had created only what he alone could conceive within his mind. The Apostles James declares:

> *From whence come wars and fightings among you? come they not hence, even of your lusts that war in your members? Ye lust, and have not: ye kill, and desire to have, and cannot obtain: ye fight and war, yet ye have not, because ye ask not. Ye ask, and receive not, because ye ask amiss, that ye may consume it upon your lusts.* (James 4:1-3)

4:8	And Cain talked with Abel his brother: and it came to pass, when they were in the field, that Cain rose up against Abel his brother, and slew him.
4:9	And the Lord said unto Cain, Where is Abel thy brother? And he said, I know not: Am I my brother's keeper?
4:10	And he said, What hast thou done? the voice of thy brother's blood crieth unto me from the ground.

Here we find a clue as to what caused Cain's anger and rage. Cain's question, *'Am I my brother's keeper?'* shows what was in his mind that led to the resentment and rage that resulted in a murder. Was it fair that Cain should toil to produce the grass that fattened his brother's sheep while his brother was rewarded for simply offering what the earth had produced through Cain's toiling? Was it fair for Cain to be his brother's keeper and not be rewarded for effort? Although Adam had warned Cain of sin's power, his anger turned to resentment, then to rage, and finally murder. One can be angry without committing sin:

Be ye angry, and sin not: let not the sun go down upon your wrath (Ephesians 4: 26).

Unfortunately Cain's anger conceived the sin that led to the first murder recorded in scripture. Cain's anger, rage and subsequent murderous act was not the result of an inherited sinful nature, but the result of his failure to recognise that it is wrong to submit to the power of jealousy and resentment that too often ends in violence. Cain was described by Jesus as *'your father, the devil, who was a murderer from the beginning'* (John 8:44). Although many accept the traditional view that Jesus was referring to a literal devil, clearly it was Can whom Jesus referred to as 'a murderer from the beginning'.

4:11   And now art thou cursed from the earth, which hath opened her mouth to receive thy brother's blood from thy hand;

4:12   When thou tillest the ground, it shall not henceforth yield unto thee her strength; a fugitive and a vagabond shalt thou be in the earth.

4:13   And Cain said unto the Lord, My punishment is greater than I can bear.

4:14   Behold, thou hast driven me out this day from the face of the earth; and from thy face shall I be hid; and I shall be a fugitive and a vagabond in the earth; and it shall come to pass, that every one that findeth me shall slay me.

4:15   And the Lord said unto him, Therefore whosoever slayeth Cain, vengeance shall be taken on him sevenfold. And the Lord set a mark upon Cain, lest any finding him should kill him.

4:16   And Cain went out from the presence of the Lord, and dwelt in the land of Nod, on the east of Eden.

4:17   And Cain knew his wife; and she conceived, and bare Enoch: and he builded a city, and called the name of the city, after the name of his son, Enoch.

Cain could no longer remain in one place for fear of being persecuted and perhaps killed. He knew the unprecedented murder of his own brother would not go unnoticed amongst those already occupying the banks of the rivers. Cain also knew the predicament he was in and fearful for his life, therefore he could no longer settle in one place and appreciate the earth's full potential. The loss he felt had driven him to despair and grief.

Immediately after Cain had killed his brother, his countenance had fallen. Cain was a murderer from the beginning and father of all who were to breach the law of love. He admitted that his punishment was more than he could bear; thus his disposition was noticeably different than those out in the earth. He had no choice but to mingle amongst those who could easily attack and possibly kill him because of their suspicions and fear of a stranger.

The 'mark' of Cain expresses fear and insecurity, typical of those who resort to hatred and violence rather than love and gentleness. The sons of God already occupying the earth had no reason to exhibit fear or guilt.

> *For this is the message that ye heard from the beginning, that we should love one another. Not as Cain, who was of that wicked one, and slew his brother. And wherefore slew he him? Because his own works were evil, and his brother's righteous* (1 John 3: 11-12).

> *Ye are of your father the devil, and the lusts of your father ye will do. He was a murderer from the beginning, and abode not in the truth, because there is no truth in him. When he speaketh a lie, he speaketh of his own: for he is a liar, and the father of it* (John 8:44).

When Jesus said to Peter, 'get behind me Satan', he was not referring to a satanic being, but of Peter's countenance that revealed his doubts and unbelief.

> *Then Peter took him, and began to rebuke him, saying, Be it far from thee, Lord: this shall not be unto thee. But he turned, and said unto Peter, Get thee behind me, Satan: thou art an offence unto me: for thou savourest not the things that be of God, but those that be of men* (Matthew 16: 22-23).

Peter was rebuked not because he was concerned for Jesus, but because he was more concerned for his own welfare endangered by his association with Jesus. Soon after this event, Peter betrayed Jesus by denying that he was his disciple. It wasn't as serious as murder, but Peter did prove to be a 'liar'. If Cain was a 'murderer and a liar', then Peter rightfully deserved being called 'Satan' since he was savouring the things of men rather than God.

Cain by now was dwelling in the land of Nod east of Eden where he chose a wife from amongst the existing tribes along the four rivers mentioned in Genesis 2. After the birth of Enoch, Cain is not mentioned again until the birth of Lamech (Genesis 4:24). The reference to '*he built a city*' immediately after Enoch is mentioned does not necessarily mean that Cain was the builder. If Cain was afraid for his life, he most likely would not have put himself in such a vulnerable position building a city. It's more likely that Cain was the architect who named the city after his son once he was old enough to build a city to protect his father from any who may seek to take his father's life. Whatever the case, Cain's descendants are the first on record that built a city.

Men of great intellect and ability built structures and monuments that surpass to some extent what we can achieve today with modern technology and machinery. We should never underestimate the legacy left by the descendants of Cain. Unlike the descendants of Seth, Cain's descendants worshipped many gods. The Apostle Paul speaks of this time when men worshipped 'birds, four footed animals, and creeping things (Romans 1:20-32). It is possible that many of the ancient structures still with us today were once closer together but had drifted from their original geographical locations when the single land mass separated into the islands and continents we have today.

4:18 And unto Enoch was born Irad: and Irad begat Mehujael: and Mehujael begat Methusael: and Methusael begat Lamech.

The names of the descendants of Cain and Seth have striking similarities. While Enoch is the son of Cain and grandson of Adam, Seth's third time removed grandson is also named Enoch, a fourth removed grandson of Adam who 'walked with God' (Genesis 5:24). Cain's descendants, although having similar names, did not necessarily walk with God as did Seth's descendants.

4:19 And Lamech took unto him two wives: the name of the one was Adah, and the name of the other Zillah.

4:20 And Adah bare Jabal: he was the father of such as dwell in tents, and of such as have cattle.

4:21 And his brother's name was Jubal: he was the father of all such as handle the harp and organ.

4:22 And Zillah, she also bare Tubalcain, an instructer of every artificer in brass and iron: and the sister of Tubalcain was Naamah.

Although nothing is mentioned about the origins of Adah and Zillah, the skills and gifts of their offspring are evident to this day with the likes of agriculture, music, and manufacturing various metals and resources of the earth. Jabal was a farmer while his brothers were gifted with skills in making musical instruments. Tubalcain's hand was skilful with manufacturing and shaping things in brass and iron. Of interest, there is no mention of Seth's descendants having skills with musical instruments or with manufacturing artefacts in brass and iron; nevertheless in both Cain's and Seth's descendants we have gifts and talents that have originated through the mingling of seed between mankind and Adam's descendants.

Farming involves harvest time and celebration with music and praise. Here we see two biological brothers with gifts that complement harvest time and celebration. Tubalcain, not the least important of the three, may have shaped the ploughs and tools from brass and iron that helped with Jabal's gift in agriculture. Whatever the case, those gifts that originated during the ages of antiquity are still with us today. While things of brass, iron, and other metals have helped for the good of humanity with manufacturing food, clothing, household goods, vehicles, and so on, those metals are also used for manufacturing instruments of war for the cause of evil.

4:23   And Lamech said unto his wives, Adah and Zillah, Hear my voice; ye wives of Lamech, hearken unto my speech: for I have slain a man to my wounding, and a young man to my hurt.

4:24   If Cain shall be avenged sevenfold, truly Lamech seventy and sevenfold.

According to the genealogies of Genesis 5, Lamech's great-great-great-grandfather Cain was still alive and reasonably young when he confessed '*I have slain a man to my wounding and a young man to my hurt*'. Of further interest, according to the genealogies in Chapter 5, Seth was around five hundred and fifty-seven years of age when Enoch, the seventh from Adam, was born. This may indicate that Lamech, the seventh from Cain, was around the same age. Seeing that Lamech was the seventh from Adam on Cain's side, the sevenfold curse was possibly pointing to Lamech as the one who killed Cain. Being a descendant of a fugitive and vagabond may have caused Lamech some grief, and as a result, Lamech may have murdered Cain.

> 4:25 And Adam knew his wife again; and she bare a son, and called his name Seth: For God, said she, hath appointed me another seed instead of Abel, whom Cain slew.

After focusing on the life of Cain and his descendants, the narrative abruptly turns back to Adam and Eve. Exactly when Eve gave birth to Seth in relation to the timeline of Cain and his descendants is not clear. The term 'another seed instead of Abel' suggests that no children were born between Cain and Seth. That Adam knew his wife 'again' doesn't suggest a hit-and-miss conception; Adam purposely 'knew his wife again' so they could bear another child 'instead' of Abel whom Cain had slain.

> 4:26 And to Seth, to him also there was born a son; and he called his name Enos: then began men to call upon the name of the Lord.

Once again we find that Seth, like Cain, had found a wife with no explanation of her origin. The traditional view that God allowed Cain to choose a sister is typical of how things can be invented to suit the narratives if there is seemingly no other explanation.

> *As also in all his epistle, speaking in them of these things; in which are some things hard to be understood, which they that are unlearned and unstable wrest, as they do also the other scriptures, unto their own destruction (2 Peter 3:16).*

Consider the following; if Adam and Eve produced other offspring besides Abel, Cain, and Seth, why hadn't those offspring called on the name of the Lord? It was only from the time Enos was born that men began to call on the name of the Lord. Obviously those described in Genesis 1:26 hadn't called on the name of the Lord because there was no one amongst them who could be called Lord. The narrative is clear that both Cain and Seth had many women to choose from amongst those out in the earth. Although those described in Genesis 1:26 were created in the image and likeness of God, they later fell victims to their carnal passions. Because of the offspring born from the union between mankind and the offspring of Adam and Eve, the children from this union produced women that were 'more fair and beautiful', hence the men got carried away with their sexual lust for those women (Genesis 6:1,2).

Although the Apostle Paul's description below is specifically speaking about the condition of those back then who had yielded to their carnal natures, there have been stages throughout history, including this present generation showing strikingly similar characteristics of those who ignore their divine consciousness.

> *For the invisible things of him from the creation of the world are clearly seen, being understood by the things that are made, even his eternal power and Godhead; so that they are without excuse: Because that, when they knew God, they glorified him not as God, neither were thankful; but became vain in their imaginations, and their foolish heart was darkened. Professing themselves to be wise, they became fools, And changed the glory of the uncorruptible God into an image made like to corruptible man, and to birds, and four-footed beasts, and creeping things. Wherefore God also gave them up to uncleanness through the lusts of their own hearts, to dishonour their own bodies between themselves: Who changed the truth of God into a lie, and worshipped and served the creature more than the Creator, who is blessed forever. Amen. For this cause God gave them up unto vile affections: for even their women did change the natural use into that which is against nature: And likewise also the men, leaving the natural use of the woman, burned in their lust one toward another; men with men working that which is unseemly, and receiving in themselves that recompense of their error which was meet. And even as they did not like to retain God in their knowledge, God gave them over to a reprobate mind, to do those things which are not convenient; Being filled with all unrighteousness, fornication, wickedness, covetousness, maliciousness; full of envy, murder, debate, deceit, malignity; whisperers, Backbiters, haters of God,*

despiteful, proud, boasters, inventors of evil things, disobedient to parents, Without understanding, covenant breakers, without natural affection, implacable, unmerciful: Who knowing the judgment of God, that they which commit such things are worthy of death, not only do the same, but have pleasure in them that do them. (Romans 1:20-32).

GENESIS CHAPTER 5

5:1   This is the book of the generations of Adam. In the day that God created man, in the *likeness* of God made he him;

5:2   Male and female created he them; and blessed them, and called their name Adam, in the day when they were created.

5:3   And Adam lived an hundred and thirty years, and begat a son in his own likeness, and after his image; and called his name Seth:

Notice here that the 'man' is in the 'likeness' of God, and not both 'likeness and image' of God. The 'man', later named Adam had only 'become' like God in both image and likeness since Eve also had her eyes opened to the knowledge of good and evil (Genesis 3:22). When the sons of Adam had chosen wives from amongst the existing tribes, they were blessed and named 'Adam'. This union should not be confused with those from Genesis 1:26-28 that were commanded to be fruitful, multiply, and replenish the earth. They are nameless and without genealogies. The book of 'the generations of Adam' are those who called on 'the name of the Lord' (Genesis 4:26). Adam at the time was the Lord of every male and female born through Seth's descendants that called on his name. Had Eve chosen not to open her eyes, there would be no generations of Adam to speak of. Here we see the genealogies working back from Joseph through the ages to Enos, Seth, and Adam, the Son of God.

Which was the son of Enos, which was the son of Seth, which was the son of Adam, which was the son of God (Luke 3:38).

In Seth we have an example of children born in the likeness and image of their parents, whether immediate offspring or third and fourth generation grandchildren. Seth is described here as one in the *'likeness and after the image'* of his father Adam. In this example we learn that through the gift of procreation, the seed preserves the likeness from where the likeness first springs.

5:4   And the days of Adam after he had begotten Seth were eight hundred years: and he begat sons and daughters:

5:5   And all the days that Adam lived were nine hundred and thirty years: and he died.

5:6   And Seth lived an hundred and five years, and begat Enos:

5:7   And Seth lived after he begat Enos eight hundred and seven years, and begat sons and daughters:

5:8   And all the days of Seth were nine hundred and twelve years: and he died.

5:9   And Enos lived ninety years, and begat Cainan:

5:10 And Enos lived after he begat Cainan eight hundred and fifteen years, and begat sons and daughters:

5:11 And all the days of Enos were nine hundred and five years: and he died.

5:12 And Cainan lived seventy years and begat Mahalaleel:

5:13 And Cainan lived after he begat Mahalaleel eight hundred and forty years, and begat sons and daughters:

5:14 And all the days of Cainan were nine hundred and ten years: and he died.

5:15 And Mahalaleel lived sixty and five years, and begat Jared:

5:16 And Mahalaleel lived after he begat Jared eight hundred and thirty years, and begat sons and daughters:

5:17 And all the days of Mahalaleel were eight hundred ninety and five years: and he died.

5:18 And Jared lived an hundred sixty and two years, and he begat Enoch:

5:19 And Jared lived after he begat Enoch eight hundred years, and begat sons and daughters:

5:20 And all the days of Jared were nine hundred sixty and two years: and he died.

5:21 And Enoch lived sixty and five years, and begat Methuselah:

5:22 And Enoch walked with God after he begat Methuselah three hundred years, and begat sons and daughters:

5:23 And all the days of Enoch were three hundred sixty and five years:

5:24 And Enoch walked with God: and he was not; for God took him.

5:25 And Methuselah lived an hundred eighty and seven years, and begat Lamech.

5:26 And Methuselah lived after he begat Lamech seven hundred eighty and two years, and begat sons and daughters:

5:27 And all the days of Methuselah were nine hundred sixty and nine years: and he died.

5:28 And Lamech lived an hundred eighty and two years, and begat a son:

5:29 And he called his name Noah, saying, This same shall comfort us concerning our work and toil of our hands, because of the ground which the Lord hath cursed.

5:30 And Lamech lived after he begat Noah five hundred ninety and five years, and begat sons and daughters:

5:31 And all the days of Lamech were seven hundred seventy and seven years: and he died.

5:32 And Noah was five hundred years old: and Noah begat Shem, Ham, and Japheth.

The age of each descendant at the time of their firstborn is on record to show that men once fathered children at an average age of more than a hundred years. Although the average life span is over seventy years, it appears there will be a day when the average life span will be much longer. Notice the words from Isaiah when speaking about longer life and lasting peace on earth.

> *There shall be no more thence an infant of days, nor an old man that hath not filled his days: for the child shall die an hundred years old; but the sinner being an hundred years old shall be accursed. And they shall build houses, and inhabit them; and they shall plant vineyards, and eat the fruit of them. They shall not build, and another inhabit; they shall not plant, and another eat: for as the days of a tree are the days of my people, and mine elect shall long enjoy the work of their hands. They shall not labour in vain, nor bring forth for trouble; for they are the seed of the blessed of the Lord, and their offspring with them. And it shall come to pass, that before they call, I will answer; and while they are yet speaking, I will hear. The wolf and the lamb shall feed together, and the lion shall eat straw like the bullock: and dust shall be the serpent's meat. They shall not hurt nor destroy in all my holy mountain, saith the Lord* (Isaiah 65:20-25).

The Apostle Paul states a similar hope for the world to come.

> *But as it is written, Eye hath not seen, nor ear heard, neither have entered into the heart of man, the things which God hath prepared for them that love God (1 Corinthians 2:9).*

The phrase 'Enoch was not' illustrates the great faith and hope placed in the promises of God. Genesis is not saying that Enoch had avoided dying a natural death and was miraculously transported somewhere beyond this world. Jesus had clarified this thousands of years since Enoch; *'no one has ascended to heaven but he who came down from heaven': that is, the Son of Man who is in heaven* (John 3:14). If Enoch was literally taken to heaven, here was an opportune time for Jesus to speak about Enoch's literal ascension. The number seven is significant because it symbolises a completion of God's creative works in both the natural and spiritual world. According to the scriptures there were fourteen generations from Abraham to David, followed by fourteen generations from David to Israel's captivity in Babylon, and finally another fourteen generations to Jesus Christ, a cycle of a thousand years and multiples of sevens (Matthew 1:17). Enoch was the seventh generation from Adam, the number that represents the completeness of Enoch's testimony and what he had accomplished in his life before the world went through a transformation.

> *By faith Enoch was translated that he should not see death; and was not found, because God had translated him: for before his translation he had this testimony, that he pleased God* (Hebrews 11:5).

Enoch was the first descendant to be given a vision of what was to be humanity's pivotal point in history. He did not 'see death' because he knew that through the promised seed he was guaranteed everlasting life. That 'he was not found' simply implies that his death and burial was not recorded, nor the place of his burial ever found. He went to sleep and waited for his rebirth through the seed of his descendants. Enoch is an example of all who go to their graves and remain asleep until they enter life again.

Observe that both Cain and Abel are excluded from the genealogies. Abel at the time of his death had no offspring; therefore there are no descendants of Abel to speak of. Cain's children are not included in Luke's ancestral line from Jesus to Adam since he was separated from his immediate family because of Abel's death.

Name	Age at birth of son	Years lived after birth of son	Age at death
Adam	130 (Seth)	800	930
Seth	105 (Enos)	807	912
Enos	90 (Cainan)	815	905
Cainan	70 (Mahalaleel)	840	910
Mahaleleel	65 (Jared)	836	895
Jared	162 (Enoch)	800	962
Enoch	65 (Methuselah)	300	365
Methuselah	187 (Lamech)	782	969
Lamech	182 (Noah)	595	777
Noah	500 (Ham, Shem, Japeth)	450	950

GENESIS CHAPTER 6

6:1   And it came to pass, when men began to multiply on the face of the earth, and daughters were born unto them,

6:2   That the sons of God saw the daughters of men that they were fair; and they took them wives of all which they chose.

6:3   And the Lord said, My spirit shall not always strive with man, for that he also is flesh: yet his days shall be an hundred and twenty years.

6:4   There were giants in the earth in those days; and also after that, when the sons of God came in unto the daughters of men, and they bare children to them, the same became mighty men which were of old, men of renown.

6:5   And God saw that the wickedness of man was great in the earth, and that every imagination of the thoughts of his heart was only evil continually.

6:6   And it repented the Lord that he had made man on the earth, and it grieved him at his heart.

The New Testament Book of Jude sheds a great deal of light on the origin of the sons of God and what had led to their sexual immorality. They are described in the Book of Jude as *'angels that kept not their first estate'*, because they were created in the likeness and image of God and knew the difference between good and evil.

The New Testament describes that evil generation this way:

Jude

> *And the angels which kept not their first estate, but left their own habitation, he hath reserved in everlasting chains under darkness unto the judgment of the great day.* (Jude 1: 6).

Romans

> *For the invisible things of him from the creation of the world are clearly seen, being understood by the things that are made, even his eternal power and Godhead; so that they are without excuse: Because that, when they knew God, they glorified him not as God, neither were thankful; but became vain in their imaginations, and their foolish heart was darkened. Professing themselves to be wise, they became fools, And changed the glory of the uncorruptible God into an image made like to corruptible man, and to birds, and fourfooted beasts, and creeping things. Wherefore God also gave them up to uncleanness through the lusts of their own hearts, to dishonour their own bodies between themselves:* (Romans 1:20-27)

2 Peter

> *For Christ also hath once suffered for sins, the just for the unjust, that he might bring us to God, being put to death in the flesh, but quickened by the Spirit: By which also he went and preached unto the spirits in prison; Which sometime were disobedient, when once the longsuffering of God waited in the days of Noah, while the ark was a preparing, wherein few, that is, eight souls were saved by water* (1 Peter 3: 18-20).

> *For if God spared not the angels that sinned, but cast them down to hell, and delivered them into chains of darkness, to be reserved unto judgment; And spared not the old world, but saved Noah the eighth person, a preacher of righteousness, bringing in the flood upon the world of the ungodly* (2 Peter 2: 4-5).

Cain and Seth produced many offspring with the women they had chosen from amongst the tribes living along the banks of the four rivers (Genesis 2:10-13). Contrary to what many believe, neither Peter, Jude, nor Paul refer to demons or aliens visiting our planet and impregnating the women described here as 'fair'. This change resulted from the unions between the offspring of Cain and Seth and the women of those already occupying the earth. The 'sons of God' were those described in Genesis 1:26-28 created in the image and likeness of God but later chose not to retain their knowledge of God.

6:7   And the Lord said, I will destroy man whom I have created from the face of the earth; both man, and beast, and the creeping thing, and the fowls of the air; for it repenteth me that I have made them.

6:8   But Noah found grace in the eyes of the Lord.

6:9   These are the generations of Noah: Noah was a just man and perfect in his generations, and Noah walked with God.

6:10 And Noah begat three sons, Shem, Ham, and Japheth.

6:11 The earth also was corrupt before God, and the earth was filled with violence.

6:12 And God looked upon the earth, and, behold, it was corrupt; for all flesh had corrupted his way upon the earth.

6:13 And God said unto Noah, The end of all flesh is come before me; for the earth is filled with violence through them; and, behold, I will destroy them with the earth.

Adam's descendants by now were genetically related to the rest of mankind through the line of Noah's three sons, Ham, Shem and Japheth, and their respective wives. Here we see procreation continuing through Noah's offspring as cousins (Genesis 10: 1-32).

There are a few possibilities with regard to the record of the flood. If it was global and all life besides Noah and his family perished, then the entire population of the mixed races of mankind, including many descendants of Adam, came to an abrupt end. Yet within the blood of every person living today is the genetic makeup of all the descendants of Adam and their offspring, including the races from amongst mankind who had mingled their blood with Adam's offspring. However, if the earth was once a single continent, the 'breaking up of the fountains of the deep' may be an indication that when the single continent was divided, remnants from the mixed races were saved (Genesis 7:11). The saving of 'eight souls' may possibly relate only to those who were preserved specifically for the calling together of Israel through the seed of Abraham's descendants.

In summary, the nations that existed before the flood:

1. The four distinct and separate races dwelling beside the four rivers created in 'the image and likeness of God' and called 'the sons of God' (Genesis 1:26-28. Genesis 6:2).

2. Children born from Seth and Cain because of the union with the women they chose from amongst those already living out on the earth (Genesis 4: 17, 26. Genesis 1:26-28).

3. The 'giants' and 'men of renown': those born from the unions between the sons of God and Seth and Cain's descendants, also referred to as 'the daughters of men' (Genesis 6:4).

4. The children of Adam and Eve after the birth of Seth.

The Genesis commentary ends with Genesis 6:13 since it contains the record of Adam's descendants until what appears to be a cataclysmic end of the ancient world. As for the descendants of Noah's sons and the offspring that had re-settled throughout the new world, the final part of this book will address what the author believes is a direct link between the nations of the world today and the original races that occupied the four rivers mentioned in Genesis 2.

Matthew 24

1. And Jesus went out, and departed from the temple: and his disciples came to him for to shew him the buildings of the temple.

2. And Jesus said unto them, See ye not all these things? verily I say unto you, There shall not be left here one stone upon another, that shall not be thrown down.

3. And as he sat upon the mount of Olives, the disciples came unto him privately, saying, Tell us, when shall these things be? and what shall be the sign of thy coming, and of the end of the world?

4. And Jesus answered and said unto them, Take heed that no man deceive you.

5. For many shall come in my name, saying, I am Christ; and shall deceive many.

6. And ye shall hear of wars and rumours of wars: see that ye be not troubled: for all these things must come to pass, but the end is not yet.

7. For nation shall rise against nation, and kingdom against kingdom: and there shall be famines, and pestilences, and earthquakes, in divers places.

8. All these are the beginning of sorrows.

In this chapter Jesus speaks exclusively of events to mark the destruction of Jerusalem. The 'sign' of Christ's coming and 'the end of the world' are precursors to an understanding of the Apostle John's Revelation of Jesus Christ. Jesus' teachings and parables shed much light on the imagery and symbolic meaning of John's visions that point to the finished work of Jesus Christ that saw the beginning of constructing a spiritual 'New Jerusalem'. Abraham spoke of this day:

> *For he looked for a city which hath foundations, whose builder and maker is God* (Hebrews 11:10).

Very few had understood what Jesus had meant when he said; *destroy this temple, and in three days I will raise it up* (John 2:19). Many were offended by his words because they at first thought he was speaking about the destruction of Herod's temple. Jesus had said:

> *In my Father's house are many mansions: if it were not so, I would have told you. I go to prepare a place for you* (John 14:2).

This is not speaking about one enormous physical mansion with smaller physical mansions within, but a single spiritual temple with members that are themselves temples within the spiritual 'body of Christ' (1 Corinthians 3:16-17).

> *And I saw a new heaven and a new earth: for the first heaven and the first earth were passed away; and there was no more sea. And I John saw the holy city, New Jerusalem, coming down from God out of heaven, prepared as a bride adorned for her husband. And I heard a great voice out of heaven saying, Behold, the tabernacle of God is with men, and he will dwell with them, and they shall be his people, and God himself shall be with them, and be their God* (Revelation 21:1-3).

The traditional view that Mathew 24 speaks of a literal and physical return of Jesus thousands of years beyond the generation he was speaking with, contradicts everything Jesus taught about the end of the world and beginning of constructing a spiritual kingdom in the 1st century AD.

The expectation of a Christ child was fundamental, not just within Judaism, but within most religions of the Middle East, especially during the first century. Language and symbolism that described deities, virgin births, crucifixion, resurrection, were common amongst worshippers who revered many gods, and sons of gods. The word 'Christos' is the Greek translation of the Hebrew 'messias' which describes one who is 'anointed'. The title was later used by early believers to distinguish Jesus as the Christ and those who falsely claimed to be the Christ of God. Whether or not the term 'Christos' was borrowed because of its intrinsic value, Paul nevertheless vigorously claims that Jesus was *'made of the seed of David, according to the flesh'* and was undoubtedly the one that was the fulfilment of the prophecies about the coming messiah (Romans 1:3). However, having the knowledge and revelation of Christ was not without risk. The faith and endurance of the infant church, even when faced with persecution and death, did not go unnoticed.

Although the Apostle Paul spoke of the 'coming' or 'appearance' of Christ as a 'revelation', many today are of the opinion that the second coming of Jesus is to be a physical appearance. However, Paul is clear throughout his epistle that Christ is not something that can be seen but what is revealed from within.

> *'But the righteousness which is of faith speaketh on this wise, Say not in thine heart, Who shall ascend into heaven? (that is, to bring Christ down from above:) Or, Who shall descend into the deep? (that is, to bring up Christ again from the dead.) But what saith it? The word is nigh thee, even in thy mouth, and in thy heart: that is, the word of faith, which we preach'* (Romans 10:6,7,8)

> *But I certify you, brethren, that the Gospel which was preached of me is not after man. For I neither received it of man, neither was I taught it, but by the revelation of Jesus Christ* (Galatians 1:11, 12).

Most would argue that the reason Jesus hadn't returned within the first century and centuries that followed was due to the Christians not being ready. However, Jesus here clarifies that the generation he was speaking to was to witness the fulfilment of all prophecies spoken of throughout the Old Testament. Everything that was written by the prophets about the finished work of redemption was about to be fulfilled: Observe:

> *God, who at sundry times and in divers manners spake in time past unto the fathers by the prophets, Hath in these last days spoken unto us by his Son, whom he hath appointed heir of all things, by whom also he made the worlds* (Hebrews 1:1-2).

The imminent revelation of Christ was echoed within the first century, not as something conditional, but what was to '*shortly come to pass*' before the end of the first century. The very title of the last book of the Bible is named the 'revelation' of Jesus Christ.

> *The Revelation of Jesus Christ, which God gave unto him, to shew unto his servants things which must shortly come to pass; and he sent and signified it by his angel unto his servant John* (Revelation 1:1).

> *Blessed is he that readeth, and they that hear the words of this prophecy, and keep those things which are written therein: for the time is at hand* (Revelation 1:3)

> *Behold, I come quickly: blessed is he that keepeth the sayings of the prophecy of this book* (Revelation 22:7)

> *And he saith unto me, Seal not the sayings of the prophecy of this book: for the time is at hand* (Revelation 22:10).

> *And, behold, I come quickly; and my reward is with me, to give every man according as his work shall be* (Revelation 22:12).

> *He which testifieth these things saith, Amen. Even so, come, Lord Jesus* (Revelation 22:20).

It is interesting that the book of Hebrews outlines the transition from all that was based on law to all that would become spiritual and based on faith and grace through Jesus Christ. Jesus had explained to his disciples there was no use looking above for a future physical coming since '*the Kingdom of God is within you*' (Luke 17:21). Paul had raised the same concerns with the Thessalonians because many were not sure if Jesus Christ had already returned. Had the coming of Christ been literal and visible and accompanied by actual lightning and trumpet sounds, Paul would not have needed to explain the following;

> *Now we beseech you, brethren, by the coming of our Lord Jesus Christ, and by our gathering together unto him, That ye be not soon shaken in mind, or be troubled, neither by spirit, nor by word, nor by letter as from us, as that the day of Christ is at hand. Let no man deceive you by any means: for that day shall not come, except there come a falling away first, and that man of sin be revealed, the son of perdition; Who opposeth and exalteth himself above all that is called God, or that is worshipped; so that he as God sitteth in the temple of God, shewing himself that he is God. Remember ye not, that, when I was yet with you, I told you these things? And now ye know what withholdeth that he might be revealed in his time. For the mystery of iniquity doth already work: only he who now letteth will let, until he be taken out of the way. And then shall that Wicked be revealed, whom the Lord shall consume with the spirit of his mouth, and shall destroy with the brightness of his coming* (2 Thessalonians 2:2-8)

As noted in the introduction of this book, a counterfeit church had begun in Paul's day. The 'coming of the Son of Man' is also likened by Jesus as a brightness compared only to *'lightning that shines from east to west'*. When one experiences a revelation of Christ, it is the 'brightness' of the knowledge of Christ that exposes everything that is falsely taught by man.

---

9. Then shall they deliver you up to be afflicted, and shall kill you: and ye shall be hated of all nations for my name's sake.

10. And then shall many be offended, and shall betray one another, and shall hate one another.

11. And many false prophets shall rise, and shall deceive many.

12. And because iniquity shall abound, the love of many shall wax cold.

13. But he that shall endure unto the end, the same shall be saved.

14. And this Gospel of the kingdom shall be preached in all the world for a witness unto all nations; and then shall the end come.

Everything Jesus had spoken and warned of, had occurred between AD 30 and AD 70. Many followers of Paul and the Apostles had abandoned their faith due to the persecution and death threats they endured. John's visions also highlight in imagery and symbols what the followers of Jesus and the Apostles endured for their faith.

The 'world' at this time was comprised of the immediate regions within Asia Minor. For example, Paul mentions in the book of Romans:

> *First, I thank my God through Jesus Christ for you all, that your faith is spoken of throughout the whole world.* (Romans 1:8)

Many with first-hand teachings from Jesus were amongst the founders who took the gospel message to the world. This was the time in history that saw the beginning of the 'church of the firstborn' which grew from a little village within Judea and spread into the known world (Hebrews 12:23).

---

15. When ye therefore shall see the abomination of desolation, spoken of by Daniel the prophet, stand in the holy place, (whoso readeth, let him understand:)

16. Then let them which be in Judaea flee into the mountains:

17. Let him which is on the housetop not come down to take any thing out of his house:

18. Neither let him which is in the field return back to take his clothes.

19. And woe unto them that are with child, and to them that give suck in those days!

20. But pray ye that your flight be not in the winter, neither on the sabbath day:

21. For then shall be great tribulation, such as was not since the beginning of the world to this time, no, nor ever shall be.

The Old Testament prophet Daniel gave a dire warning about the Jew's rejection of Christ. Daniel had predicted that the religion based on law would become an 'abomination' that would finally come to an abrupt end. Jesus crucifixion marked the end of all the Old Testament prophecies about the promise of putting an end to the Jews' transgressions and offering a remedy for their sins. Above all, it marked the time that would introduce 'everlasting righteousness', not by law keeping but by faith through God's grace. It is the 'everlasting righteousness' of Christ that is at the heart of the Old Testament writings of the prophet Daniel;

> *Seventy weeks are determined upon thy people and upon thy holy city, to finish the transgression, and to make an end of sins, and to make reconciliation for iniquity, and to bring in everlasting righteousness, and to seal up the vision and prophecy, and to anoint the most Holy* (Daniel 9:24).

To say that 'this generation' is referring to those living millennia after the destruction of Jerusalem contradicts the clear and explicit testimonies and teachings of the Apostles about the nearness of Christ. Everything that Jesus and the previous prophets had spoken of had a fulfilment within the generation that Jesus was here addressing (Revelation 1:1, 3, 7, 19; Revelation 22:7, 12, 20; Hebrews 1:2). Throughout each century, doomsday prophets have emerged from all walks of life, many of whom started new sects and cults based on the misunderstanding of Jesus and the Apostles meaning of 'the end of the world'.

22. And except those days should be shortened, there should no flesh be saved: but for the elect's sake those days shall be shortened.

23. Then if any man shall say unto you, Lo, here is Christ, or there; believe it not.

24. For there shall arise false Christs, and false prophets, and shall shew great signs and wonders; insomuch that, if it were possible, they shall deceive the very elect.

25. Behold, I have told you before.

26. Wherefore if they shall say unto you, Behold, he is in the desert; go not forth: behold, he is in the secret chambers; believe it not.

27. For as the lightning cometh out of the east, and shineth even unto the west; so shall also the coming of the Son of man be.

28. For wheresoever the carcase is, there will the eagles be gathered together.

Jeremiah spoke of the day when the knowledge of Christ would be revealed throughout the world. He predicted that the time would come when there would be such a transformation within the minds and hearts of believers there would be no further need for religious instruction.

> *But this shall be the covenant that I will make with the house of Israel; After those days, saith the Lord, I will put my law in their inward parts, and write it in their hearts; and will be their God, and they shall be my people. And they shall teach no more every man his neighbour, and every man his brother, saying, Know the Lord: for they shall all know me, from the least of them unto the greatest of them, saith the Lord: for I will forgive their iniquity, and I will remember their sin no more* (Jeremiah 31:33, 34).

Both Jeremiah and Jesus were speaking about a spiritual renewal. Jesus had warned that wherever eagles are seen circling and hovering in one place, something is about to die and be devoured. Likewise, when the Roman army circled and destroyed the city of Jerusalem, it marked not only the end of law and religion, but the day when Christ was revealed. No one knew the day or the hour of judgment that would befall Jerusalem. The Day of the Lord was to herald the death of a religion that represented law. When Christ was revealed, it was an awakening likened to 'lightning shining from east to west'.

---

29.   Immediately after the tribulation of those days shall the sun be darkened, and the moon shall not give her light, and the stars shall fall from heaven, and the powers of the heavens shall be shaken:

The Old Testament Book of Joel speaks of both tragedy and joy following Jerusalem's destruction and the dispersion of Israel. When the city was destroyed, it was as though the heavenly lights went out and darkness covered the land. Confusion, doubt, despair, and a sense of hopelessness at this time overcame the inhabitants of Jerusalem. A once proud city now lay in ruins. Within this city the prophets were stoned and mocked and their messages and warnings rejected. The Jews through their own ignorance once again experienced the final 'desolation' prophesied by Daniel centuries earlier (Daniel 9:27).

Forty years previously the disciples were shaken and distressed when all hope in Jesus seemed to have come to an abrupt end. Those who expected victory through physical force by a military king like David were bitterly disappointed, while those with the knowledge of Christ had experienced a 'revelation' and therefore rejoiced when they realised that a New Jerusalem was now ready for construction. When Titus invaded Jerusalem, it was likened to the sun, moon, and stars losing their radiance, and as though heaven itself was shaken. Then, like a repeat of the disappointment that had turned to joy forty years earlier when it was thought that Jesus had lost the victory, their disappointment once again turned to joy when they realised that Jesus had prophesied this day. It was now time to build a New Jerusalem and spiritual temple where all nations, people and tongues could worship in spirit and in truth.

30. And then shall appear the sign of the Son of man in heaven: and then shall all the tribes of the earth mourn, and they shall see the Son of man coming in the clouds of heaven with power and great glory.

31. And he shall send his angels with a great sound of a trumpet, and they shall gather together his elect from the four winds, from one end of heaven to the other.

The appearance of the Son of Man is described here as a 'sign' rather than a literal visible appearance. The 'clouds of heaven' symbolize everything that stands for the 'former and latter rain' that brings the harvest. The 'tribes of the earth' are the tribes of Israel mourning because the destruction of Jerusalem was something unimaginable. In the wake of the city's destruction, those with the faith of Jesus gathered together as one united body of faith. They are described here as 'angels' since being gathered from each corner of the known world to carry the gospel message.

32. Now learn a parable of the fig tree; When his branch is yet tender, and putteth forth leaves, ye know that summer is nigh:

33. So likewise ye, when ye shall see all these things, know that it is near, even at the doors.

34. Verily I say unto you, This generation shall not pass, till all these things be fulfilled.

35. Heaven and earth shall pass away, but my words shall not pass away.

36. But of that day and hour knoweth no man, no, not the angels of heaven, but my Father only.

This discourse was a specific warning to those living within and around Jerusalem while Titus and his Roman army gathered on the plains of Megiddo, commonly known as Armageddon[2]. To argue that 'all these things' Jesus spoke about here are yet to be fulfilled is to ignore the historical evidence of wars, famines, pestilences, and earthquakes that were prevalent during the first century. From the time Jesus uttered these prophetic words until forty years later, many factional parties and zealots that opposed being controlled by Rome actually caused the turmoil that prompted the invasion. The disciples, along with the Jews that had rejected Jesus, were warned to flee the city or suffer the consequences. When the Roman army had invaded Jerusalem it was 'a time of trouble' that had never been witnessed. The figurative 'heaven and earth' that was to 'pass away' denotes the change from what was once the worship of God within physical temples and synagogues that had connected heaven and earth through law and ceremonies, now replaced with the worship of God in spirit and in truth' (John 4:24).

37. But as the days of Noah were, so shall also the coming of the Son of man be.

38. For as in the days that were before the flood they were eating and drinking, marrying and giving in marriage, until the day that Noe entered into the ark,

39. And knew not until the flood came, and took them all away; so shall also the coming of the Son of man be.

Jesus' day did not differ from the days of Noah with greed, envy, violence, unfaithfulness, decadence, and so on. When Jerusalem was surrounded by the Roman army, the fear was not unlike those who scoffed at Noah's warning. Jesus had warned there would be 'gnashing of teeth' once the occupants of Jerusalem realised it

---

[2] The Roman army under the command of Titus actually *gathered his army together* at a place just outside of Jerusalem known in Hebrew as Armageddon. There was no such battle at Armageddon, but the gathering of the Roman legions before Titus invaded and totally destroyed Jerusalem in 70 A.D. '*And he **gathered them together** into a place called in the Hebrew tongue Armageddon*' (Revelation 16:16).

was too late to escape. Clearly the apocalyptic ending of the old Jerusalem was something unique only to the Jews. If the above verse is to be taken literally, then one would have to say that the world will end with a flood (verse 39). A symbolic 'flood' is mentioned again in John's Revelation when describing the figurative woman that was 'carried away' by a figurative flood that was a false gospel based on law. (Revelation 12:15).

40. Then shall two be in the field; the one shall be taken, and the other left.

41. Two women shall be grinding at the mill; the one shall be taken, and the other left.

Many Christian sects believe the 'one that is taken' and 'the other left', describes some kind of a 'secret rapture'. One minute you're here, the next minute you're not, as though vanishing into thin air. This conclusion is born once again from a misunderstanding of the New Testament's figurative language. Jesus used many similar parables such as 'sheep' on his right hand, and 'goats' on his left, along with other biblical 'two by two' figurative descriptions that differentiate between right and wrong (1 Chronicles 26:12,17. Mark 6:7).

42. Watch therefore: for ye know not what hour your Lord doth come.

43. But know this, that if the goodman of the house had known in what watch the thief would come, he would have watched, and would not have suffered his house to be broken up.

44. Therefore be ye also ready: for in such an hour as ye think not the Son of man cometh.

The 'signs of the times' that doomsday prophets often refer to, are a combination of 'signs and wonders' wrongly interpreted from the Old Testament Book of Daniel believed by many to go hand in hand with John's Revelations. Daniel and the Revelations, along with Mathew and Luke's gospels, plus a selection of epistles such as 1st and 2nd Peter that speak of 'the last days' are often used as proof that 'the great tribulation' is yet to come. The figurative descriptions are often slotted in wherever there have been significant events in the past and present. To this day, many sects and self appointed prophets have tried and failed to predict coming events supposed to be signs of 'the time of the end'. However, when studied in light of the biblical principle *'precept upon precept, line upon line, here a little, there a little'*, there can only be one conclusion concerning the time of 'the great tribulation'(Isaiah 28:10). The mistaken belief that the 'appearance' or 'coming of Christ' is a physical coming has led to many false interpretations.

---

45. Who then is a faithful and wise servant, whom his lord hath made ruler over his household, to give them meat in due season?

46. Blessed is that servant, whom his lord when he cometh shall find so doing.

47. Verily I say unto you, That he shall make him ruler over all his goods.

48. But and if that evil servant shall say in his heart, My lord delayeth his coming;

49. And shall begin to smite his fellowservants, and to eat and drink with the drunken;

50. The lord of that servant shall come in a day when he looketh not for him, and in an hour that he is not aware of,

51. And shall cut him asunder, and appoint him his portion with the hypocrites: there shall be weeping and gnashing of teeth.

Jesus is here reiterating the importance of staying humble and faithful and not to get too complacent with worldly things that will distract from the real issues. The whole point of Jesus' discourse was to offer Israel hope beyond the destruction of their city and temple. During these forty years there were many who scoffed at the idea that the time of the end was getting nearer and nearer, hence the blessings for all who were to take heed and flee the city as the signs became apparent. Religion and law were to be cleansed by a fire that was a melting of religious corruption at the centre of Jerusalem. Jesus' sacrifice had marked 'the end of the world' and beginning of a new found faith.

> *For then must he often have suffered since the foundation of the world: but now once in the end of the world hath he appeared to put away sin by the sacrifice of himself* (Hebrews 9:26).

THE REVELATION OF JESUS CHRIST
REVELATION 1

While a minority of scholars are of the view that John's visions were written between 54 and 68 A.D seeing that the temple at Jerusalem was still standing during the time of the visions (Revelation 11:1, 2), most scholars are convinced of a later date between 95 and 100 AD. Whatever the case, it is most likely that if the visions were written before 70 AD, what John was told to 'write' was kept out of sight but passed on by word of mouth fearing persecution. Whether the words were penned after or before the destruction of Jerusalem, the great tribulation which marked the end of the world and predicted by Jesus from the Mount of Olives had been fulfilled well before the end of the first century as evidenced by Jesus testimony from Mathew 24 and John's testimony herein; *'the time is at hand'*, and *'things which must shortly come to pass'*.

1:1 The Revelation of Jesus Christ, which God gave unto him, to shew unto his servants things which must shortly come to pass; and he sent and signified it by his angel unto his servant John:

1:2	Who bare record of the word of God, and of the testimony of Jesus Christ, and of all things that he saw.
1:3	Blessed is he that readeth, and they that hear the words of this prophecy, and keep those things which are written therein: for the time is at hand.

These visions are directly related to the 'revelation of Jesus Christ'. As the Apostle Paul confirms with John:

For I neither received it from man, nor was I taught it, but it came through the revelation of Jesus Christ (Galatians 1:12).

The revelation of Christ is not something to be learned through the teaching of men, but what is revealed through the spirit and Word of God.

But ye have not so learned Christ; If so be that ye have heard him, and have been taught by him, as the truth is in Jesus: (Ephesians 4:23).

The knowledge and revelation of Jesus Christ gave the early church the courage and strength to endure threats of persecution and death. We can now look back and understand why it was said; *Blessed is he that readeth, and they that hear the words of this prophecy, and keep those things which are written: for the time is at hand.* The members of the firstborn church knew that what they were about to accomplish would establish the foundation for a permanent temple and 'dwelling place of God' here on earth. Had John revealed in plain language the true identity of the powers at play, the church would have suffered even further persecution. The visions were expressed in symbolisms so there would be no cause for the religious and political enemies to be further concerned.

The revelation of Christ within the hearts and minds of believers gradually unfolded in the manner that Jesus had taught his disciples. *First; the blade, then the ear, then the full corn in the ear'* (Mark 4:28). First, we hear the word, then digest the word, and then we understand the word. From the Mount of Olives, Jesus had taught the parable of the scattered seed followed by the analogy in which the Kingdom of God is likened to a minuscule mustard seed that grows into one of the largest of all trees that spreads its branches as shade for all (Mark 4:1-20).

The *things which must shortly come to pass* were imminent. The message was to sound as a trumpet, just as it was before an important announcement was made on behalf of a king. Here we read of a warning to those about to be persecuted for their testimony and faith. *The time is at hand* is echoed in the first and last chapters of this book and echoed by Jesus, Paul, and the Apostles. John's visions hold the promise that the entire world will eventually become one universal body of faith, a unified spiritual place where all who love righteousness will dwell from generation to generation forever and ever.

> *But ye are come unto mount Sion, and unto the city of the living God, the heavenly Jerusalem, and to an innumerable company of angels, To the general assembly and church of the firstborn, which are written in heaven, and to God the Judge of all, and to the spirits of just men made perfect, And to Jesus the mediator of the new covenant, and to the blood of sprinkling, that speaketh better things than that of Abel* (Hebrews 12:22-24).

Although the visions show what was 'shortly to take place', the believers' triumph and final victory was certain. Expressions such as *the time is at hand, things which must shortly come to pass, behold I come quickly*, were addressed to those who gathered together to prepare for the appearance of Christ, not in a bodily form, but as a revelation (1 Thessalonians 2:19, 20:1; Thessalonians 2:1, 2:2; Thessalonians 5:1-7). Jesus had reminded his audience of Daniel's prophetic warnings about the fate of those in Jerusalem. It prompted him to say, *Let them who be in Judaea flee into the mountains* (Matthew 24:16). Both believing and unbelieving Jews were about to endure what Jesus had predicted to be 'a time of trouble such as never was'. Although *'the beginning of sorrows'* would cause many to lose their first love, others would endure and remain faithful to the end; therefore, *for the elect's sake, those days were shortened* (Matthew 24:8-22).

Like a woman in labour before childbirth, the early church experienced extreme pain before and during the time of the end.

The devastation of this once glorious city symbolically named in John's revelation as 'Sodom and Egypt', was the focal point of the Day of Judgment (Revelation 11:8). Old Jerusalem with its earthly temple was about to become a carcass, a symbolic dead body where eagles would gather and dispose of its remains. In the wake of Jerusalem's destruction, *a New Jerusalem came down from heaven, prepared as a bride adorned for her husband*' (Revelation 21:2). Those with 'the faith of Jesus' were getting ready to adorn themselves symbolically with the righteousness of Christ, so they might forever remain citizens within the figurative New Jerusalem.

> *But this I say, brethren, the time is short: it remaineth, that both they that have wives be as though they had none; And they that weep, as though they wept not; and they that rejoice, as though they rejoiced not; and they that buy, as though they possessed not; And they that use this world, as not abusing it: for the fashion of this world passeth away* (1 Corinthians 7: 29-31)

> *And the world passeth away, and the lust thereof: but he that doeth the will of God abideth for ever. Little children, it is the last time: and as ye have heard that Antichrist shall come, even now are there many Antichrists; whereby we know that it is the last time* (1 John 2:17,18)

1:4 John to the seven churches which are in Asia: Grace be unto you, and peace, from him which is, and which was, and which is to come; and from the seven Spirits which are before his throne;

Paul, the most prolific writer of all the Apostles, sent seven letters to seven churches with messages of encouragement to those about to be persecuted for their faith. The seven letters addressed by the Apostle Paul: Romans, Corinthians, Galatians, Ephesians, Philippians, Colossians, and Thessalonians, were messages of comfort and admonition. Each of Paul's letters correspond with the messages to the seven churches. The letters reveal the strengths and weaknesses that describe the spiritual state of each church. It is interesting to note that Paul's letters to the seven churches bear striking similarities with the issues outlined in John's vision.

> **1:5** And from Jesus Christ, who is the faithful witness, and the first begotten of the dead, and the prince of the kings of the earth. Unto him that loved us, and washed us from our sins in his own blood,

At the heart of John's visions is the revelation of Christ, and why it could only be Jesus who could be called *the first begotten of the dead*. As already examined in Genesis, the *first* Adam was a natural man formed at the beginning and the same man who appeared again as the *last* Adam in the fullness of the Christ of God;

> *For unto which of the angels said he at any time, Thou art my Son, this day have I begotten thee? And again, I will be to him a Father, and he shall be to me a Son? And again, when he bringeth in the firstbegotten into the world, he saith, And let all the angels of God worship him* (Hebrews 1:5, 6).

This very contentious argument that the first and last Adam is one identical Son of God may be ridiculed for now, but the time will come when Christianity will have to come to terms with the truth about Adam. The first Adam was *the beginning of the creation of God* within humanity, *the firstborn of all creation* (Revelation 3:14. Colossians 1:15-19). The first and last Adam is the *alpha* and the *omega* of our salvation. The first Adam, to this day, is accused of bringing sin into the world, even though the Apostle Timothy explicitly states that *Adam was not deceived* (1 Timothy 2:14. Genesis 3:22. Luke 3:38).

> *And so it is written, The first man Adam was made a living soul; the last Adam was made a quickening spirit. Howbeit that was not first which is spiritual, but that which is natural; and afterward that which is spiritual. The first man is of the earth, earthy; the second man is the Lord from heaven. As is the earthy, such are they also that are earthy: and as is the heavenly, such are they also that are heavenly. And as we have borne the image of the earthy, we shall also bear the image of the heavenly.* (1 Corinthians 15 45-49).

1:6	And hath made us kings and priests unto God and his Father; to him be glory and dominion for ever and ever. Amen.

Between Paul's letters is an Epistle that bears no record of the author, but simply named 'Hebrews'. It may well have been written by Paul due to the detailed description of the old covenant based on law, and the new covenant based on grace. The book of Hebrews has a broader message for the Gentile world regarding the finished work of Christ Jesus as high priest. Here we see in John's first vision, all who are 'in Christ' and have the faith of Jesus are ordained as priests. The true church has no further use for an earthly priesthood since every believer is a priest of God forever (1 Peter 4:7, Hebrews 9:26).

> *But ye are a chosen generation, a royal priesthood, an holy nation, a peculiar people; that ye should shew forth the praises of him who hath called you out of darkness into his marvellous light* (1 Peter 2:9).

1:7	Behold, he cometh with clouds; and every eye shall see him, and they also which pierced him: and all kindreds of the earth shall wail because of him. Even so, Amen.

The shapes and colours of clouds in the evening often indicate what the weather will be like the following day. The description here of 'clouds' was to remind Jesus' hearers of what was imminent (Luke 12:56). As Jesus had said, there would appear the 'sign' of the Son of man coming in the 'clouds of heaven with power and glory' (Matthew 24:30). Jesus had spoken about signs that would indicate the nearness of the Day of Judgment, a time when the Roman armies would fall upon Jerusalem and 'every eye', including the eyes of 'those that pierced him', would grieve and lament. Jesus' warning was about to reach its prophetic fulfilment when he warned that the time was near and even at the door.

> **1:8** I am Alpha and Omega, the beginning and the ending, saith the Lord, which is, and which was, and which is to come, the Almighty.

The Alpha and the Omega is called the Almighty, because Christ, the Word of God, is both creator and redeemer. Christ is the omniscience that now dwells within humanity.

> *Who is the image of the invisible God, the firstborn of every creature: For by him were all things created, that are in heaven, and that are in earth, visible and invisible, whether they be thrones, or dominions, or principalities, or powers: all things were created by him, and for him: And he is before all things, and by him all things consist. And he is the head of the body, the church: who is the beginning, the firstborn from the dead; that in all things he might have the preeminence. For it pleased the Father that in him should all fullness dwell* (Colossians 1:15-19).

As already noted from Genesis, on the third day the forming of Adam from the earth was the beginning of the creation of God within humanity.

> *That which was from the beginning, which we have heard, which we have seen with our eyes, which we have looked upon, and our hands have handled, of the Word of life; (For the life was manifested, and we have seen it, and bear witness, and shew unto you that eternal life, which was with the Father, and was manifested unto us;) That which we have seen and heard declare we unto you, that ye also may have fellowship with us: and truly our fellowship is with the Father, and with his Son Jesus Christ. And these things write we unto you, that your joy may be full* (1 John 1:1-4).

> **1:9** I John, who also am your brother, and companion in tribulation, and in the kingdom and patience of Jesus Christ, was in the isle that is called Patmos, for the word of God, and for the testimony of Jesus Christ.

Whether John was aware he would be chosen to give such a powerful testimony before being exiled to Patmos, is not certain. The testimony of Jesus was especially for those about to go through the trials that would teach patience while waiting for Christ to be revealed.

The Apostles were the first to learn the meaning of 'the kingdom and patience of Jesus Christ', and mindful there had never been one who bore the 'express image' of God as was evident within the person and character of Jesus. They each had learned from their experiences that tribulation develops patience.

1:10   I was in the Spirit on the Lord's day, and heard behind me a great voice, as of a trumpet,

---

This was the day in which the fulfilment of all the Old Testament prophecies relating to the revelation and coming of Christ were fulfilled. It was the day that Abraham had looked forward to, and the time that marked the beginning of those who would be declared 'righteous' without the deeds of the law. This was the day when reconciliation between man and God was accomplished by Christ Jesus who would bring together all the nations of the world under one banner of faith.

All the previous patriarchs and prophets such as Noah, Job, Daniel, Jeremiah, Isaiah, Ezekiel, David, and a host of others, died hoping this day would be a reality. This day was ordained from the beginning when God had 'rested' from all the created works. It is the 'rest' we find in Christ moment by moment. The Lord's Day is the substance of what was once only a shadow of the true rest (Genesis 2:1, 2). The voice 'as of a trumpet' is the prophetic utterance that warned of the imminent fall of Jerusalem. The trumpets symbolised the word of God to be preached throughout Asia Minor. Jesus spoke of this time when he said:

> *And he shall send his angels with a great sound of a trumpet, and they shall gather together his elect from the four winds, from one end of heaven to the other* (Matthew 24:31).

The Revelation of Jesus Christ - Revelation 1

1:11   Saying, I am Alpha and Omega, the first and the last: and, What thou seest, write in a book, and send it unto the seven churches which are in Asia; unto Ephesus, and unto Smyrna, and unto Pergamos, and unto Thyatira, and unto Sardis, and unto Philadelphia, and unto Laodicea.

1:12   And I turned to see the voice that spake with me. And being turned, I saw seven golden candlesticks;

1:13   And in the midst of the seven candlesticks one like unto the Son of man, clothed with a garment down to the foot, and girt about the paps with a golden girdle.

1:14   His head and his hairs were white like wool, as white as snow; and his eyes were as a flame of fire;

1:15   And his feet like unto fine brass, as if they burned in a furnace; and his voice as the sound of many waters.

1:16   And he had in his right hand seven stars: and out of his mouth went a sharp two edged sword: and his countenance was as the sun shineth in his strength.

John here depicts the contrast between what is 'earthly' and what is 'heavenly'. The 'earthly' sanctuary was temporary and based on an earthly priesthood under law, while the new 'heavenly' sanctuary is permanent and based on 'Christ, the end of the law for righteousness'. Jesus is here depicted as the high priest because he not only kept the commandments perfectly, but taught the importance of what the 'spirit of the law' requires. Jesus is walking in the midst of the seven candlesticks because the candles represent the light given to the Apostles. The light was extended to the Gentiles via the Apostles along with Paul's letters to the seven churches along with the seven other letters to and from Timothy, Titus, Philemon, James, Peter, John, Jude.

1:17   And when I saw him, I fell at his feet as dead. And he laid his right hand upon me, saying unto me, Fear not; I am the first and the last:

1:18	I am he that liveth, and was dead; and, behold, I am alive for evermore, Amen; and have the keys of hell and of death.
1:19	Write the things which thou hast seen, and the things which are, and the things which shall be hereafter;

Jesus here reiterates that he is the *first* and the *last*, the author and finisher of our faith. The image of the Son of man holding the keys of 'hell and death' is not depicting a literal hell, but the kingdoms of evil within this world. It is up to the individual whether one is born in a 'heavenly place' or in a place likened to hell on earth. As long as humanity pursues good rather than evil, there will be less evidence of hell on earth. The final chapter of John's vision describes two classes of people; those within the New Jerusalem and those outside the New Jerusalem. We are born either within the body of Christ or outside the body of Christ, there is no in between. It cannot be overstated enough that we are either 'asleep', 'dead', or 'alive' to Christ.

1:20	The mystery of the seven stars which thou sawest in my right hand, and the seven golden candlesticks. The seven stars are the angels of the seven churches: and the seven candlesticks which thou sawest are the seven churches.

Each of the seven Epistles to and from Timothy, Titus, Philemon, James, Peter, John, and Jude, reveal the character of those Apostles. All who are righteous and heavenly minded are 'angels'. Paul compares Timothy's genuine faith with the same faith and character he saw in his mother Eunice and grandmother Lois, while Titus is described by Paul as 'my own son after the common faith' (2 Timothy 2:5; Titus 1:4). Philemon is described as a man so full of love and faith, and that his very presence was refreshing (Philemon 1:1-7). Jude is described as one unmoved when confronted with unholy men, and one who kept a 'holy faith', while James, Peter, and John had the humility and compassion to reach out to the poor. Angels exist today in all walks of life as ordinary, everyday people who care for their neighbours and friends with no expectations of reward.

REVELATION 2

2:1 Unto the angel of the church of Ephesus write; These things saith he that holdeth the seven stars in his right hand, who walketh in the midst of the seven golden candlesticks;

2:2 I know thy works, and thy labour, and thy patience, and how thou canst not bear them which are evil: and thou hast tried them which say they are Apostles, and are not, and hast found them liars:

2:3 And hast borne, and hast patience, and for my name's sake hast laboured, and hast not fainted.

2:4 Nevertheless I have somewhat against thee, because thou hast left thy first love.

2:5 Remember therefore from whence thou art fallen, and repent, and do the first works; or else I will come unto thee quickly, and will remove thy candlestick out of his place, except thou repent.

2:6 But this thou hast, that thou hatest the deeds of the Nicolaitanes, which I also hate.

2:7 He that hath an ear, let him hear what the Spirit saith unto the churches; To him that overcometh will I give to eat of the tree of life, which is in the midst of the paradise of God.

The seven stars depict the seven angels of the New Testament. Paul is the first of the seven angels' messages of the New Testament. It was Paul to whom Jesus appointed to preach the meaning of Christ. Jesus is here holding the seven stars that represent the Epistles that Paul addressed to the seven churches. Ephesus at the time was the second largest city of the Roman Empire and most accessible, especially as a platform for Paul's preaching.

Religion flourished to the extent that both Rome and Ephesus became centres for debating philosophy and religion. Although Paul's core message was focused on Christ, many were being drawn back to keeping the law as a means of righteousness and salvation. This message was not only for Ephesus, but for all future generations to not get caught up in law (Ephesians 1: 3-5). Paul's awakening and subsequent revelation of Christ is evident in his letter to the Ephesians. However, at Ephesus and Rome, Paul encountered opposition, particularly from Jews who could not comprehend that the righteousness of Christ could be given freely without the need for circumcision or need to follow the letter of the law.

The Nicolaitans zealously taught that righteousness can only be attained through circumcision and by law keeping. They also had restrictions about what one should eat and how one should keep the Sabbath and other 'deeds of the law' rather than accepting Jesus' teaching about justice and mercy as it relates to the spirit of the law. Many argue that Paul and James were in disagreement over faith and works, but both had no misgivings about how faith and love work together. Both Paul and James agree on the spirit of the law, and both agree that when one has 'the faith of Jesus' it is impossible to sit on one's hands and do nothing.

John is here reminded of the importance of holding fast to the faith and not losing one's first love because of the cares of this world. The tree of life is a reminder of eternal life through the gift of love and procreation. Through the seed of regeneration we are raised again to remain within the body of Christ forever and ever (1 John 3:9). Although the congregations scattered around Asia Minor were once spiritually alive and 'raised together' in the heavenly places in

Christ, they had lost their first love and enthusiasm in sharing their knowledge of Christ with others (Ephesians 2:5, 6, 7).

2:8   And unto the angel of the church in Smyrna write; These things saith the first and the last, which was dead, and is alive;

2:9   I know thy works, and tribulation, and poverty, (but thou art rich) and I know the blasphemy of them which say they are Jews, and are not, but are the synagogue of Satan.

2:10 Fear none of those things which thou shalt suffer: behold, the devil shall cast some of you into prison, that ye may be tried; and ye shall have tribulation ten days: be thou faithful unto death, and I will give thee a crown of life.

2:11 He that hath an ear, let him hear what the Spirit saith unto the churches; He that overcometh shall not be hurt of the second death.

Believers are here reminded that even when faced with persecution and death, the resurrection of life within the spiritual body of Christ is guaranteed. The term 'second death' is used here to draw attention to a 'death' that is powerless over those who belong to Christ.

Satan is not a depiction of a literal devil, but figurative of the political and religious powers that tried to silence the early church. Jesus once had to use the term 'Satan' to teach Peter that the source of evil is not from something external but what comes from within:

But he turned, and said unto Peter, Get thee behind me, Satan: thou art an offence unto me: for thou savourest not the things that be of God, but those that be of men (Matthew 16:23).

The very mention of the word 'synagogue' and 'Satan' shows how those opposing the early believers while operating within their respective religious powers, were in union with the political powers, and vice versa. Here again we are reminded that through Christ we may have the victory over fear and victory over the second death.

The mention of 'ten days' symbolises a very short time of suffering, whereas in later chapters 'months' and 'years' symbolise longer periods.

2:12   And to the angel of the church in Pergamos write; These things saith he which hath the sharp sword with two edges;

2:13   I know thy works, and where thou dwellest, even where Satan's seat is: and thou holdest fast my name, and hast not denied my faith, even in those days wherein Antipas was my faithful martyr, who was slain among you, where Satan dwelleth.

2:14   But I have a few things against thee, because thou hast there them that hold the doctrine of Balaam, who taught Balac to cast a stumbling block before the children of Israel, to eat things sacrificed unto idols, and to commit fornication.

2:15   So hast thou also them that hold the doctrine of the Nicolaitanes, which thing I hate.

2:16   Repent; or else I will come unto thee quickly, and will fight against them with the sword of my mouth.

2:17   He that hath an ear, let him hear what the Spirit saith unto the churches; To him that overcometh will I give to eat of the hidden manna, and will give him a white stone, and in the stone a new name written, which no man knoweth saving he that receiveth it.

The 'throne of Satan' was Jerusalem itself. It was the city in which Jesus wielded a two-edged sword that had exposed the hypocrisy of the religious leaders and their pretentious piety. The foremost enemy of Jesus and his followers was not the Roman Empire, but his own countrymen. The early believers had suffered persecution at the hands of Nero and others, even though the persecution was mostly confined to the area around Judea. The guardians of the Jewish religion throughout Asia Minor relentlessly persecuted believers such as Antipas and Stephen and Jesus. Rome may have permitted the execution of Jesus under Pilate, but the power of the Pharisees ultimately plotted Jesus' death.

Although the Jewish religious parties opposed each other, the rival factions were of one mind and eventually silenced Jesus by accusing him of sedition and blasphemy.

Since Rome had no jurisdiction or interest over charges of blasphemy unless it was against Caesar, and although Pontius Pilate was bound as a magistrate to order the execution, he nevertheless washed his hands after admitting he could find no fault with Jesus (Mathew 27:24,25). Although Paul and the Apostles suffered at the hands of the Pharisees and almost suffered the same fate as Antipas and Stephen, Paul nevertheless clarified by both word and letter that regardless of the opposition from within his own nation, victory in Christ was assured. Those being persecuted by the enemy had therefore found comfort in both Paul's letters and John's revelations.

The 'hidden manna' is a figurative expression of the knowledge of Christ that had been hidden through the ages. The 'manna' is the 'bread of life' offered to all. On the night before the crucifixion, Jesus invited the disciples to take the bread and eat, as a memorial and symbol of the 'word of life' (Colossians 1:26).

2:18 And unto the angel of the church in Thyatira write; These things saith the Son of God, who hath his eyes like unto a flame of fire, and his feet are like fine brass;

2:19 I know thy works, and charity, and service, and faith, and thy patience, and thy works; and the last to be more than the first.

2:20   Notwithstanding I have a few things against thee, because thou sufferest that woman Jezebel, which calleth herself a prophetess, to teach and to seduce my servants to commit fornication, and to eat things sacrificed unto idols.

2:21   And I gave her space to repent of her fornication; and she repented not.

2:22   Behold, I will cast her into a bed, and them that commit adultery with her into great tribulation, except they repent of their deeds.

2:23   And I will kill her children with death; and all the churches shall know that I am he which searcheth the reins and hearts: and I will give unto every one of you according to your works.

2:24   But unto you I say, and unto the rest in Thyatira, as many as have not this doctrine, and which have not known the depths of Satan, as they speak; I will put upon you none other burden.

2:25   But that which ye have already hold fast till I come.

2:26   And he that overcometh, and keepeth my works unto the end, to him will I give power over the nations:

2:27   And he shall rule them with a rod of iron; as the vessels of a potter shall they be broken to shivers: even as I received of my Father.

2:28   And I will give him the morning star.

2:29   He that hath an ear, let him hear what the Spirit saith unto the churches.

Jezebel was the symbol of Israel's 'adulteries' and the ultimate symbol of refusal to embrace the faith of Jesus. Isaiah, Jeremiah, Daniel, Ezekiel and other Old Testament prophets pleaded with Israel to embrace mercy and compassion or otherwise suffer the inevitable judgment that would fall upon them. Jesus had taught that sexual desire for another man's wife is as sinful as physically committing adultery, so therefore the law is magnified when the spirit of the law is in the heart.

Paul's letters clarify the relationship between law and grace. Those who dishonour their parents, murder, fornicate, lie, covet, etc, are condemned by the law, while those who choose not to do such things are not bound by law. There are many who mistakenly believe that we cannot live without sinning so therefore we are 'law breakers' by nature from the cradle to the grave. Yet although the woman caught in the act of adultery was told, *'Go and sin no more'*, and John is clear that *'whoever is born of God does not sin'* many believe we remain in a sinful condition. (John 8:11. 1 John 5:18). What Christians need to understand is that to *'be perfect, as your Father in heaven is perfect'*, is a state of consciousness (Mathew 5:48). With our flesh we may serve the law of sin, but with the mind, we serve the law of God ((Romans 7:25). It is only within the spirit of the mind from where our Christ consciousness can be perfected.

> *There is therefore now no condemnation to them which are in Christ Jesus, who walk not after the flesh, but after the Spirit. For the law of the Spirit of life in Christ Jesus hath made me free from the law of sin and death* (Romans 8:1, 2).

The entire Book of the Revelation of Jesus Christ is all about our spiritual renewal, well being, and faith, relating to the teachings of Jesus and the Apostles about the finished work of Christ. To interpret John's vision and revelation of Christ any other way, is to lose sight of the present reality of the Kingdom of God. A spiritual dwelling place for God was established almost two thousand years ago as a permanent structure. Although it is an ongoing construction being built by the members of Christ, those who walk, not after the flesh, but after the spirit, will find comfort and strength within its walls, (figuratively speaking).

REVELATION 3

3:1 And unto the angel of the church in Sardis write; These things saith he that hath the seven Spirits of God, and the seven stars; I know thy works, that thou hast a name that thou livest, and art dead.

3:2 Be watchful, and strengthen the things which remain, that are ready to die: for I have not found thy works perfect before God.

3:3 Remember therefore how thou hast received and heard, and hold fast, and repent. If therefore thou shalt not watch, I will come on thee as a thief, and thou shalt not know what hour I will come upon thee.

3:4 Thou hast a few names even in Sardis which have not defiled their garments; and they shall walk with me in white: for they are worthy.

3:5 He that overcometh, the same shall be clothed in white raiment; and I will not blot out his name out of the book of life, but I will confess his name before my Father, and before his angels.

3:6 He that hath an ear, let him hear what the Spirit saith unto the churches.

Paul's encouragement to those who had doubts about the time of Jesus' coming is reiterated here in John's vision. To those who were distressed about their personal and individual lives, Paul had advised them to remain as they were, seeing that the time of Jesus' reappearance was near:

> *Art thou bound unto a wife? seek not to be loosed. Art thou loosed from a wife? seek not a wife. But and if thou marry, thou hast not sinned; and if a virgin marry, she hath not sinned. Nevertheless such shall have trouble in the flesh: but I spare you. But this I say, brethren, the time is short: it remaineth, that both they that have wives be as though they had none; And they that weep, as though they wept not; and they that rejoice, as though they rejoiced not; and they that buy, as though they possessed not; And they that use this world, as not abusing it: for the fashion of this world passeth away* (1 Corinthians 7: 27-31).

Jesus had warned his generation:

> *And woe unto them that are with child, and to them that give suck in those days! But pray ye that your flight be not in the winter, neither on the sabbath day: For then shall be great tribulation, such as was not since the beginning of the world to this time, no, nor ever shall be* (Matthew 24:19-21).

Israel and the inhabitants of Jerusalem were called to embrace the faith of Jesus and carry the light of the gospel to the nations of the world, but instead ignored the message of God's grace and plotted the arrest of Jesus and subsequently had him shamefully crucified. In this chapter we see those amongst Judaism who opposed the message of grace. Instead they zealously tried to convince those who followed the Apostles advice that the only way to be saved was by law keeping. The testimony of Christ Jesus was about to be confirmed within a short time:

> *I thank my God always on your behalf, for the grace of God which is given you by Jesus Christ; That in everything ye are enriched by him, in all utterance, and in all knowledge; Even as the testimony of Christ was confirmed in you: So that ye*

> *come behind in no gift; waiting for the coming of our Lord Jesus Christ: Who shall also confirm you unto the end, that ye may be blameless in the day of our Lord Jesus Christ* (1 Corinthians 1:4-8).

Paul's language describes the spiritual state of the church before Christ was to be revealed. The letters to the seven churches were specifically written as a warning to those who were tempted to return back to their former ways. Many believers at the time were obviously spiritually alive to Christ while those influenced by Judaism were spiritually dead in Christ (Ephesians 5:14). Paul knew that the time was short and that 'the fashion of the world' as they knew it would pass away once Jerusalem was destroyed. Jesus had warned that although the time was imminent, many would be 'sleeping' (1 Corinthians 7:30, 31. Matthew 25:5).

In this vision John reminds us of Jesus' teaching regarding the sudden destruction of Jerusalem and what would mark the revelation of Christ and 'the end of the world'. When the city was ruined along with its religion and earthly priesthood, all the warnings that Jesus had spoken of regarding the Day of Judgment would be brought to mind. It was 'the end of the world' and the beginning of a new age when all authority was given to Christ.

> *But now once in the end of the world hath he appeared to put away sin by the sacrifice of himself* (Hebrews 9:26b).

The 'church of the firstborn' began as an infant body to grow and mature as the 'body of Christ' that was now alive and within the world. This was now the time of restitution, a time when the 'new heavens' and a 'new earth' would be revealed. Wherever Paul or any other Apostle speaks of Christ sitting at the right hand of God, they are not speaking about an external physical being sitting on a throne within a literal temple, but the spiritual temple of God within this world. To imagine that God's dwelling place is in a faraway place somewhere out in the universe contradicts the clear testimony that God's dwelling place is now within the body of humanity.

> *Know ye not that ye are the temple of God, and that the Spirit of God dwelleth in you?* (1 Corinthians 3:16).

Jesus' discourse of Mathew 24 speaks of the 'sign of the Son of man', while Paul also explains the manner and timing when Christ was to be revealed (Thessalonians 2:1-4). Paul admonished those planning courtship and marriage to reconsider because of what they would have to endure before, and in the wake of the city's destruction (1 Corinthians 7:26-31). The letters to the seven churches reveal much about Paul's frustrations with the Jew's opposition to Christ.

The *'white raiment'* that is given to the saints and those who were to follow, symbolised the righteousness of Christ without 'the deeds of the law'.

3:7   And to the angel of the church in Philadelphia write; These things saith he that is holy, he that is true, he that hath the key of David, he that openeth, and no man shutteth; and shutteth, and no man openeth;

3:8   I know thy works: behold, I have set before thee an open door, and no man can shut it: for thou hast a little strength, and hast kept my word, and hast not denied my name.

3:9   Behold, I will make them of the synagogue of Satan, which say they are Jews, and are not, but do lie; behold, I will make them to come and worship before thy feet, and to know that I have loved thee.

3:10   Because thou hast kept the word of my patience, I also will keep thee from the hour of temptation, which shall come upon all the world, to try them that dwell upon the earth.

3:11   Behold, I come quickly: hold that fast which thou hast, that no man take thy crown.

3:12   Him that overcometh will I make a pillar in the temple of my God, and he shall go no more out: and I will write upon him the name of my God, and the name of the city of my God, which is new Jerusalem, which cometh down out of heaven from my God: and I will write upon him my new name.

3:13   He that hath an ear, let him hear what the Spirit saith unto the churches.

Paul's teaching concerning the natural birth of Jesus 'through the seed of David according to the flesh', holds a fundamental truth about the 'key of David' (Romans 1:3, 4). In this chapter we notice the direct link between Jesus and David. The Apostle Peter also shows the inseparable link between Jesus and David (Acts 2: 17-47). In a later chapter Jesus is described as 'the root and the offspring of David' (Revelation 22:16). As already observed from Genesis, the *first* Adam is the 'root', the *alpha* of God, while the 'offspring of David' is the *last* Adam, the *omega* of God. It is therefore David, the one who appeared between the first and last Adam who holds the key to our understanding of compassion and redemption through the rebirth and resurrection of himself within the person of the baby Jesus. When Jesus uttered the words 'It is finished', the door that no man could shut or open guaranteed our rebirth within the body of Christ. The 'key of David' is the key to never-ending life. '*He shall go no more out*' simply means that life within the body of Christ is guaranteed to be everlasting. In David is the example of the resurrection of life.

While Judaism is familiar with the name YHWH, it has nevertheless failed to acknowledge Jesus who went by the Hebrew name 'Yehoshua' as the anointed Christ of God. Although the name Yehoshua is sanctified and holy, glorifying both Father and Son, the English translation for Jesus does not reflect the true meaning of the Hebrew name Yehoshua which means 'saviour'. Although many in Paul's day were claiming to be the Christ and 'deceiving even the elect', it was necessary that whenever a doubt was raised regarding the identity of the Christ, the question was asked: 'do you believe that Yehoshua is the Christ'? The name Yehoshua, or the shortened version Yeshua was associated with Christ as an acknowledgement of acceptance and belief that Yehoshua, the son of Joseph, was truly the Christ of God.

Paul was concerned for those who had 'the faith of Jesus', yet were being taught a different gospel. His letter to the congregation in Rome puts forward a convincing argument why many of the Jewish converts were going back to following the traditions of men:

> *Brethren, my heart's desire and prayer to God for Israel is, that they might be saved. For I bear them record that they have a zeal of God, but not according to knowledge. For they being ignorant of God's righteousness, and going about to establish their own righteousness, have not submitted themselves unto the righteousness of God. For Christ is the end of the law for righteousness to every one that believeth* (Romans 10:1-4).

Despite the Jews' rejection of the Christ of God, their preservation has been remarkable. Although the Jews are hated and despised by many of their neighbours, Israel as a nation remains independent even though her people are scattered throughout the world. Unfortunately many fundamentalist Christians have erroneously concluded that Israel will be at the centre of an 'end time apocalypse' not realizing that the judgment day has long passed. Fortunately for Israel, Christianity's end time mentality has played a major role in preserving the Jews through military aid and support from America, their greatest ally. Israel's glory is yet to be recognised. When the world realises how the Jews' blindness is the Gentiles' blessing, they will no longer be despised but adored even by their enemies.

3:14 **And unto the angel of the church of the Laodiceans write; These things saith the Amen, the faithful and true witness, the beginning of the creation of God;**

3:15 **I know thy works, that thou art neither cold nor hot: I would thou wert cold or hot.**

3:16　So then because thou art lukewarm, and neither cold nor hot, I will spue thee out of my mouth.

3:17　Because thou sayest, I am rich, and increased with goods, and have need of nothing; and knowest not that thou art wretched, and miserable, and poor, and blind, and naked:

3:18　I counsel thee to buy of me gold tried in the fire, that thou mayest be rich; and white raiment, that thou mayest be clothed, and that the shame of thy nakedness do not appear; and anoint thine eyes with eyesalve, that thou mayest see.

3:19　As many as I love, I rebuke and chasten: be zealous therefore, and repent.

3:20　Behold, I stand at the door, and knock: if any man hear my voice, and open the door, I will come in to him, and will sup with him, and he with me.

3:21　To him that overcometh will I grant to sit with me in my throne, even as I also overcame, and am set down with my Father in his throne.

3:22　He that hath an ear, let him hear what the Spirit saith unto the churches.

The good news of the gospel is that we have our justification, sanctification, and glorification complete in Christ. The message to the church in Laodicea reinforces the message of justification by faith alone, without the deeds of the law. Our sanctification and glorification is characterised here as 'gold purified by fire'. The trials of this life teach patience, endurance, hope, and whatever is required to form the character for the next life.

Within this life, we may live as though we already have eternal life, but it is a mistake to become complacent. By faith we may be clothed with a garment that represents the 'righteousness of Christ', not only because of our willingness to open the door and follow Christ, but to acknowledge that without Christ's righteousness humanity would remain naked and without hope. Just as Eve had her eyes opened to her nakedness by listening to the voice of reason, it is the reasoning power within the individual that exposes one's nakedness when one feels as though they are in a hopeless position.

REVELATION 4

4:1 After this I looked, and, behold, a door was opened in heaven: and the first voice which I heard was as it were of a trumpet talking with me; which said, Come up hither, and I will shew thee things which must be hereafter.

4:2 And immediately I was in the spirit: and, behold, a throne was set in heaven, and one sat on the throne.

4:3 And he that sat was to look upon like a jasper and a sardine stone: and there was a rainbow round about the throne, in sight like unto an emerald.

4:4 And round about the throne were four and twenty seats: and upon the seats I saw four and twenty elders sitting, clothed in white raiment; and they had on their heads crowns of gold.

4:5 And out of the throne proceeded lightnings and thunderings and voices: and there were seven lamps of fire burning before the throne, which are the seven Spirits of God.

Our attention is now drawn to 'one that sat on the throne', which typifies the figurative 'Father and Son' as 'one' for their beloved Israel. We are now witnessing, with John, a very important turning point regarding the fate of the Jews. Israel was a chosen nation meant to preach Christ to all the nations of the world, but since they had rejected Jesus' message, the Gentile nations were adopted, just as a branch is grafted onto the original tree and draws from the same root. Paul's letter to the Romans addresses the depth of God's desire to save Israel (Romans chapters 9, 10, 11). There remains a remnant within Israel that holds to the testimony of Jesus while remaining faithful to the Gospel of Christ. The twenty-four elders are those from amongst Judaism once in bondage to law but now praising God and wearing the robes that represent the righteousness of Christ. The seven lamps of fire are the seven spirits mentioned again to remind the reader of the importance of Paul's epistles that relate to both Jew and Gentile:

> *But Esaias is very bold, and saith, I was found of them that sought me not; I was made manifest unto them that asked not after me. But to Israel he saith, All day long I have stretched forth my hands unto a disobedient and gainsaying people* (Romans 10:20-21).

> *I say then, Hath God cast away his people? God forbid. For I also am an Israelite, of the seed of Abraham, of the tribe of Benjamin. God hath not cast away his people which he foreknew. Wot ye not what the scripture saith of Elias? how he maketh intercession to God against Israel saying, Lord, they have killed thy prophets, and digged down thine altars; and I am left alone, and they seek my life. But what saith the answer of God unto him? I have reserved to myself seven thousand men, who have not bowed the knee to the image of Baal. Even so then at this present time also there is a remnant according to the election of grace. And if by grace, then is it no more of works: otherwise grace is no more grace. But if it be of works, then it is no more grace: otherwise work is no more work. What then? Israel hath not obtained that which he seeketh for; but the election hath obtained it, and the rest were blinded* (Romans 11:1-7).

4:6   And before the throne there was a sea of glass like unto crystal: and in the midst of the throne, and round about the throne, were four beasts full of eyes before and behind.

4:7 And the first beast was like a lion, and the second beast like a calf, and the third beast had a face as a man, and the fourth beast was like a flying eagle.

4:8 And the four beasts had each of them six wings about him; and they were full of eyes within: and they rest not day and night, saying, Holy, holy, holy, Lord God Almighty, which was, and is, and is to come.

4:9 And when those beasts give glory and honour and thanks to him that sat on the throne, who liveth for ever and ever,

4:10 The four and twenty elders fall down before him that sat on the throne, and worship him that liveth for ever and ever, and cast their crowns before the throne, saying,

4:11 Thou art worthy, O Lord, to receive glory and honour and power: for thou hast created all things, and for thy pleasure they are and were created.

The sea of glass represents the peace and serenity given to those with the knowledge of Christ and 'the faith of Jesus'. Although John later mentions that 'there is no more sea', his statement does not contradict the above. The 'sea' symbolises the divisions between the nations of the world, while the 'sea and its waves' symbolise the conflict between the nations that do not have the knowledge and revelation of Christ (Luke 21:25).

The four beasts represent the characteristics of the living Word spoken by Jesus. The lion represents the power and strength of the Word when rebuking the false teaching of religion. The calf represents the gentleness of the Word of God, especially when giving hope and comfort to the poor. The face of a man is characteristic of the Son of Man who had dwelt amongst us and given his life for the world. The eagle is the symbol of the Word of God that is swift and powerful, while having an overall view of what was to be echoed throughout the world.

It is interesting to observe that Ezekiel's Old Testament account of four-winged creatures does not represent the total shift from the Old to the New Testament, whereas John's four six-winged creatures represents twenty-four elders of Israel that shows the transition from law to grace between the Old Testament and the New Testament (Ezekiel 1:4-28).

The similarities between Ezekiel's vision of the four living creatures and those of John's four beasts are noticeable. Ezekiel describes the creatures he saw in a vision as all having 'the face of a man', 'an eagle', 'the right side of the face a lion', and 'the left side of the face an ox', all of which are describing the characteristics of the Son of God. The 'lightning and thundering, sapphire, amber, burnished bronze' are similar in both Old and New Testaments, however while Ezekiel's visions relate to those under the laws of Moses, John's visions relate only to those who are saved by grace since Jesus Christ had fulfilled the law. In this vision, John is shown just how history repeats itself. The similarities between the destruction of the First Temple built by Solomon in the 10th century B.C.E. and the destruction of the Second Temple in 70 A.D. are striking. Both Ezekiel's and John's visions draw our attention to how earthly temples can only be temporary. Temples and gathering places made of stone, wood, marble, and glass, for example, are buildings that can only symbolize 'church' and God's presence. A beautiful cathedral is not the reality of the temple of God. Sacrifices and gifts placed on alters cannot appease the gods, or God for that matter. Earthly temples are simply meeting places where the words of spirit and life are preached, while the true sacrifices are the sacrifices that come from the heart.

> *For I desired mercy, and not sacrifice; and the knowledge of God more than burnt offerings* (Hosea 6:6).
>
> *But if ye had known what this meaneth, I will have mercy, and not sacrifice, ye would not have condemned the guiltless* (Mathew 12:7).

John's vision is a reminder of Ezekiel's warning about Israel's rejection of all the previous prophets. In this chapter, Israel once again wipes its hands of the last and final prophet, Jesus, hence its total destruction. Notice the following from Ezekiel.

> *And he said unto me, Son of man, stand upon thy feet, and I will speak unto thee. And the spirit entered into me when he spake unto me, and set me upon my feet, that I heard him that spake unto me. And he said unto me, Son of man, I send thee to the children of Israel, to a rebellious nation that hath rebelled against me: they and their fathers have transgressed against me, even unto this very day. For they are impudent children and stiff hearted. I do send thee unto them; and thou shalt say unto them, Thus saith the Lord God. And they, whether they will hear, or whether they will forbear, (for they are a rebellious house,) yet shall know that there hath been a prophet among them* (Ezekiel 2:1-5).

Ezekiel, like John, was given a parchment scroll to eat which at first tasted 'sweet', but later became 'bitter'. Ezekiel, along with the other Old Testament prophets had what appeared to be an impossible task in trying to convince Israel they were in danger of a fearful judgment. However, even though a final solution was offered, it was once again rejected (Ezekiel 3:1-7, 14).

The Lion from the tribe of Judah is worthy to open the scroll because Jesus had the power of a lion to defeat the enemies of the Gospel of Christ. Here we see the contrast between the Old Testament and the New Testament. The Old Testament maintains that the law must be a means of righteousness, while the New Testament points to the promise of the 'righteousness that is of faith'. In a later chapter, those who are no longer bound by law and are now walking in the spirit of the law, are heard singing 'the Song of Moses and the Song of the Lamb'. It is the song of those redeemed amongst the Israelites, celebrating Jesus' victory over the law since its curse was nailed to the cross.

> *Christ hath redeemed us from the curse of the law, being made a curse for us: for it is written, Cursed is every one that hangs on a tree* (Galatians 3:13)

Revelation 5

5:1   And I saw in the right hand of him that sat on the throne a book written within and on the backside, sealed with seven seals.

5:2   And I saw a strong angel proclaiming with a loud voice, Who is worthy to open the book, and to loose the seals thereof?

5:3   And no man in heaven, nor in earth, neither under the earth, was able to open the book, neither to look thereon.

5:4   And I wept much, because no man was found worthy to open and to read the book, neither to look thereon.

5:5   And one of the elders saith unto me, Weep not: behold, the Lion of the tribe of Judah, the Root of David, hath prevailed to open the book, and to loose the seven seals thereof.

5:6   And I beheld, and, lo, in the midst of the throne and of the four beasts, and in the midst of the elders, stood a Lamb as it had been slain, having seven horns and seven eyes, which are the seven Spirits of God sent forth into all the earth.

5:7   And he came and took the book out of the right hand of him that sat upon the throne.

> **5:8** And when he had taken the book, the four beasts and four and twenty elders fell down before the Lamb, having every one of them harps, and golden vials full of odours, which are the prayers of saints.

Our attention is again drawn to a book, only this time there are seven seals. The seals represent the letters to the seven churches, along with the seven letters to and from the Apostles. It was more than providential that when the New Testament Epistles were put together over the first few centuries, Paul's seven letters, along with the seven letters to and from the Apostles, were included. To think that Paul's epistles were approved under the guidance of such corrupt powers was nothing short of providential. In this chapter, the 'angels' of the churches are now in the spotlight.

Although the gospels of Matthew, Mark, Luke and John have played a significant role in our understanding of the life and teachings of Jesus, including Matthew and Luke's accounts of Jesus' birth, here we see the importance of the Apostles' letters that give an insight into John's visions. Without the Epistles, particularly the writings of Paul, the truth about Jesus' natural birth would not have come to light. Here we are shown that Jesus is 'the Root of David'. The only one worthy of opening the scroll is the Root and Offspring of David.

Those amongst the Jews who had listened to Paul's discourses within the churches of Ephesus, Smyrna, Pergamum, Thyatira, Sardis, Philadelphia and Laodicea, were profoundly moved by Paul's teaching of God's grace that was to be preached to every nation, kindred, and tongue. In this vision we notice that the elders acknowledge Jesus' legitimacy to his kingship.

> **5:9** And they sung a new song, saying, Thou art worthy to take the book, and to open the seals thereof: for thou wast slain, and hast redeemed us to God by thy blood out of every kindred, and tongue, and people, and nation;

5:10   And hast made us unto our God kings and priests: and we shall reign on the earth.

5:11   And I beheld, and I heard the voice of many angels round about the throne and the beasts and the elders: and the number of them was ten thousand times ten thousand, and thousands of thousands;

5:12   Saying with a loud voice, Worthy is the Lamb that was slain to receive power, and riches, and wisdom, and strength, and honour, and glory, and blessing.

5:13   And every creature which is in heaven, and on the earth, and under the earth, and such as are in the sea, and all that are in them, heard I saying, Blessing, and honour, and glory, and power, be unto him that sitteth upon the throne, and unto the Lamb for ever and ever.

5:14   And the four beasts said, Amen. And the four and twenty elders fell down and worshipped him that liveth for ever and ever.

The new song summarises the historical turning point in which all power and authority was given to Christ Jesus in gathering every nation under heaven together as one. The Amen is from the redeemed amongst the Israelites, those who acknowledged that Jesus is the Christ, the One who has received 'blessing and honour and glory and power'.

It is interesting to note that when Jesus had chosen his disciples, some were given new names. The followers of Jesus are also given 'new names' and rejoice with a new song since being delivered from bondage. Paul's letters, particularly his letter to the Galatians, shows the gratitude of finding freedom in Christ and being delivered from bondage: Observe the following from Paul's letter to the Galatians that puts the conflict between law and grace into perspective.

O foolish Galatians, who hath bewitched you, that ye should not obey the truth, before whose eyes Jesus Christ hath been evidently set forth, crucified among you? This only would I learn of you, Received ye the Spirit by the works of the law, or by the hearing of faith? Are ye so foolish? having begun in the Spirit, are ye now made perfect by the flesh? Have ye suffered so many things in vain? if it be yet in vain.

He therefore that ministereth to you the Spirit, and worketh miracles among you, doeth he it by the works of the law, or by the hearing of faith? Even as Abraham believed God, and it was accounted to him for righteousness. Know ye therefore that they which are of faith, the same are the children of Abraham.

And the scripture, foreseeing that God would justify the heathen through faith, preached before the Gospel unto Abraham, saying, In thee shall all nations be blessed. So then they which be of faith are blessed with faithful Abraham. For as many as are of the works of the law are under the curse: for it is written, Cursed is every one that continueth not in all things which are written in the book of the law to do them. But that no man is justified by the law in the sight of God, it is evident: for, The just shall live by faith.

And the law is not of faith: but, The man that doeth them shall live in them. Christ hath redeemed us from the curse of the law, being made a curse for us: for it is written, Cursed is every one that hangeth on a tree: That the blessing of Abraham might come on the Gentiles through Jesus Christ; that we might receive the promise of the Spirit through faith (Galatians 3:1-14).

REVELATION 6

6:1 And I saw when the Lamb opened one of the seals, and I heard, as it were the noise of thunder, one of the four beasts saying, Come and see.

6:2 And I saw, and behold a white horse: and he that sat on him had a bow; and a crown was given unto him: and he went forth conquering, and to conquer.

6:3 And when he had opened the second seal, I heard the second beast say, Come and see.

6:4 And there went out another horse that was red: and power was given to him that sat thereon to take peace from the earth, and that they should kill one another: and there was given unto him a great sword.

The beasts depicted in chapter four: the lion, calf, the one with a face of a man, and the flying eagle, are not separate from the four horses. There is only one rider, and that rider is Christ Jesus. The rider has a message for the white, black, red, and pale nations of the world. Although there has been much debate over the identity of the four horsemen, assumed to be symbolic of end time apocalyptic events, the connection between the colours of the horses and the colours of the nations of the world should not be overlooked. It is interesting that while describing the separate role of Adam in the Garden of Eden, the narrative is suddenly interrupted with a description of a river that flowed from Eden and through the garden, and then finally separated into four major rivers (Genesis 2: 10-14). Genesis specifically names four rivers and what may have been four separate coloured races that inhabited the banks of those rivers, namely white, red, black, and a non-descript pale colour.

The rider has a bow and crown that symbolises his former military skills and kingship as David. However, the time has now come to subdue the enemy, not with military might and a physical sword, but with the Spirit and Word of God, described here as the Sword of the Spirit. Jesus had disrupted the religious leaders by taking their peace from the earth, in the sense that the Pharisees and many of the common people were seeing that the complacency and association with the Roman Empire they were subject to was to be disrupted. In Jesus' own words to his countrymen:

Suppose ye that I am come to give peace on earth? I tell you, Nay; but rather division: For from henceforth there shall be five in one house divided, three against two, and two against three. The father shall be divided against the son, and the son against the father; the mother against the daughter, and the daughter against the mother; the mother in law against her daughter in law, and the daughter in law against her mother in law (Luke 12:51-53).

Previously from the comments of Matthew 24, Jesus warned that many would betray one another because of his message:

Then shall they deliver you up to be afflicted, and shall kill you: and ye shall be hated of all nations for my name's sake. And then shall many be offended, and shall betray one another, and shall hate one another (Matthew 24:9-10).

Before Paul had met Jesus, he was a Pharisee and zealous law keeper who had consented to the death of Stephen (Acts 7:56-60). Paul's previous law keeping and subsequent conviction about Christ had obviously made him the best choice to preach Christ as the end of the law for righteousness.

Of further interest are the first two living creatures that announce the riders of the white and red horses. Here the riders depict David and Jesus. Each is symbolised as a lion, a symbol of courage and strength in both military might and spiritual might. Likewise, both David and Jesus are symbols of a calf that can display both gentleness and courage.

6:5   And when he had opened the third seal, I heard the third beast say, Come and see. And I beheld, and lo a black horse; and he that sat on him had a pair of balances in his hand.

6:6   And I heard a voice in the midst of the four beasts say, A measure of wheat for a penny, and three measures of barley for a penny; and see thou hurt not the oil and the wine.

The third beast that has 'the face of a man' announces the rider on the black horse. The rider is depicted with a pair of scales as one given authority to judge. Christ Jesus is the only one in whom all authority and judgment was given (John 5:27). The measure of wheat for a penny, and three measures of barley for a penny is the fair and equal balance that represents the ingredients for making bread, symbolically 'the bread of life'. Without oil, the ingredients cannot be properly kneaded; therefore the spirit cannot do its work.

Observe that the rider is sent a message first to his own people and then to the four corners of the Gentile world, here represented by the one quart and the three quarts of wheat and barley. The 'bread of life' is the Word of God to be carried to the Gentiles without hurting the oil and wine, the symbol of the Holy Spirit that is 'the Comforter' (John 14:26).

6:7   And when he had opened the fourth seal, I heard the voice of the fourth beast say, Come and see.

6:8   And I looked, and behold a pale horse: and his name that sat on him was Death, and Hell followed with him. And power was given unto them over the fourth part of the earth, to kill with sword, and with hunger, and with death, and with the beasts of the earth.

The fourth beast is the flying eagle with an overview of all that is below. The name is linked with Death and Hell that followed to remind us that wrong choices will lead to a life outside the body of Christ. The rider is named Death only because those who continue to ignore their Christ consciousness will continue to condone violence and war and therefore be judged. Hell is a figurative place for those who remain in bondage to sin rather than accepting the invitation to be born again into the kingdom of light. The rider strikes fear only to those who reject Christ. This vision depicts the final destruction of the old Jerusalem, and a reminder that outside the Kingdom of God there will never be peace on earth.

6:9   And when he had opened the fifth seal, I saw under the altar the souls of them that were slain for the word of God, and for the testimony which they held:

6:10   And they cried with a loud voice, saying, How long, O Lord, holy and true, dost thou not judge and avenge our blood on them that dwell on the earth?

6:11   And white robes were given unto every one of them; and it was said unto them, that they should rest yet for a little season, until their fellowservants also and their brethren, that should be killed as they were, should be fulfilled.

Persecution of the early believers under the direction of the Pharisees and political Rome were of the most violent nature. The violence and persecution became more intense over the next forty years and extended beyond the regions of Judea. Many were slain for their testimony of Jesus and the Word of God, therefore it is understandable why those with the same threats of death enquired *'How long, O Lord, holy and true, until You judge and avenge our blood on those who dwell on the earth?'*. Those who were killed for their testimony of Jesus should never be forgotten. Christians living today who believe they are yet to go through 'the great tribulation' have forgotten that 'the church of the firstborn' has already suffered for the sake of establishing a living breathing body of Christ on earth. Christians today should also be thankful to the Jews for the privilege given to the Gentiles due to their stubbornness. Their loss was the Gentile world's gain. There is no doubt, that despite Israel's rejection of Jesus, Israel will forever be preserved by those amongst the redeemed of Israel and the Gentile world who have had Christ revealed.

> *I say then, Hath God cast away his people? God forbid. For I also am an Israelite, of the seed of Abraham, of the tribe of Benjamin. God hath not cast away his people which he foreknew. Wot ye not what the scripture saith of Elias? how he maketh intercession to God against Israel saying, Lord, they have killed thy prophets, and digged down thine altars; and I am left alone, and they seek my life. But what saith the answer of God unto him? I have reserved to myself seven thousand men, who have not bowed the knee to the image of Baal. Even so then at this present time also there is a remnant according to the election of grace* (Romans 11:1-5).

The final part of this verse shows that 'the souls under the altar' were those within Judaism who embraced the faith of Jesus. As John's visions unfold, the identity of the political and religious powers that persecuted the believers between 31 AD and 70 AD had come to light. Those who are told to 'rest a little while longer' are those of the first century that were killed for their testimony. The souls who had the courage to reject Judaism and accept the teachings of Jesus and the Apostles are depicted here as having received white robes that symbolise 'the righteousness that is of faith'.

6:12   And I beheld when he had opened the sixth seal, and, lo, there was a great earthquake; and the sun became black as sackcloth of hair, and the moon became as blood;

6:13   And the stars of heaven fell unto the earth, even as a fig tree casteth her untimely figs, when she is shaken of a mighty wind.

6:14   And the heaven departed as a scroll when it is rolled together; and every mountain and island were moved out of their places.

> 6:15 And the kings of the earth, and the great men, and the rich men, and the chief captains, and the mighty men, and every bondman, and every free man, hid themselves in the dens and in the rocks of the mountains;
>
> 6:16 And said to the mountains and rocks, Fall on us, and hide us from the face of him that sitteth on the throne, and from the wrath of the Lamb:
>
> 6:17 For the great day of his wrath is come; and who shall be able to stand?

This vision is directly linked to Jesus' discourse on the Mount of Olives about the signs that marked 'the end of the world'. The temple, religion, and economy of the Jews were 'rolled back' as a scroll, while the mountains and islands that disappeared depict all that Judaism thought was permanent. The kings of the earth and all the nations of the world are here finally under the authority of Christ.

When Jesus uttered the words 'It is finished', the veil between the holy and most holy place was torn in two. It was the time and the place that gave meaning to the Apostle Paul's and John's words that 'the form of this world' with all its desires is passing away (1 Corinthians 7:31. 1 John 2:17). The partition wall between God and humanity, with its earthly sanctuary and priesthood was always meant to be temporary. It was law keeping as a means of righteousness that had put a partition wall between God and humanity, and here we see why it was now time to bring that wall down. The language of 'earthquakes', 'stars falling to earth', 'the sun turning black', 'the moon turning red', 'the fig tree casting off its late figs', 'the mountains and islands moving out of their places' are the same figurative descriptions from Mathew 24 that depicts all that was to be shaken within Judaism.

It's interesting that whenever or wherever there is sudden destruction, calamity, or something that affects us personally, most people have a compulsion to exclaim, 'Oh, my God!' as though the brain is wired to react that way. When the Roman army suddenly besieged and destroyed Jerusalem, it was this day in history when those words were uttered, 'hide us from the face of Him'.

REVELATION 7

7:1   And after these things I saw four angels standing on the four corners of the earth, holding the four winds of the earth, that the wind should not blow on the earth, nor on the sea, nor on any tree.

7:2   And I saw another angel ascending from the east, having the seal of the living God: and he cried with a loud voice to the four angels, to whom it was given to hurt the earth and the sea,

7:3   Saying, Hurt not the earth, neither the sea, nor the trees, till we have sealed the servants of our God in their foreheads.

7:4   And I heard the number of them which were sealed: and there were sealed an hundred and forty and four thousand of all the tribes of the children of Israel.

7:5   Of the tribe of Juda were sealed twelve thousand. Of the tribe of Reuben were sealed twelve thousand. Of the tribe of Gad were sealed twelve thousand.

7:6   Of the tribe of Aser were sealed twelve thousand. Of the tribe of Nephthalim were sealed twelve thousand. Of the tribe of Manasses were sealed twelve thousand.

7:7   Of the tribe of Simeon were sealed twelve thousand. Of the tribe of Levi were sealed twelve thousand. Of the tribe of Issachar were sealed twelve thousand.

> **7:8** Of the tribe of Zabulon were sealed twelve thousand. Of the tribe of Joseph were sealed twelve thousand. Of the tribe of Benjamin were sealed twelve thousand.

All living things survive on or under the earth or within the rivers and seas. Whatever is in the sky above must eventually descend to earth. Although the elements of the earth are polluted by man's carelessness and greed, ultimately the earth will be preserved by those with a mind to do so. Mankind was given 'dominion over the earth' from the beginning, and those who appreciate the natural world, instinctively want to preserve it. There are believers and unbelievers alike who desire to preserve the earth. Individuals from all nations are working together to overcome the difficulties in 'dressing and keeping' what Adam had extended beyond Eden. In these verses, God's people are shown that they must join hands with the Gentiles under the banner of Christ in preserving the nations of the world and the earth itself.

This chapter reveals the number of those from amongst the twelve tribes of Israel, who are blessed with the seal of God's promise. The number 'one hundred and forty-four thousand' is symbolic of those amongst the actual tribes of Israel, past, present, and future, who are joined with those adopted as sons and daughters from within the spiritual Israel of God. Although this chapter was written expressly for those who were ready to die for their faith, the message remains relevant for all time. Paul's Epistles have much to say about the 'seed' and 'adoption' of those who are not true Israelites.

> *Now to Abraham and his seed were the promises made. He saith not, And to seeds, as of many; but as of one, And to thy seed, which is Christ (Galatians 3:16).*

> *Whosoever is born of God doth not commit sin; for his seed remaineth in him: and he cannot sin, because he is born of God (1 John 3:9).*

The Revelation of Jesus Christ - Revelation 7

7:9   After this I beheld, and, lo, a great multitude, which no man could number, of all nations, and kindreds, and people, and tongues, stood before the throne, and before the Lamb, clothed with white robes, and palms in their hands;

7:10 And cried with a loud voice, saying, Salvation to our God which sitteth upon the throne, and unto the Lamb.

7:11 And all the angels stood round about the throne, and about the elders and the four beasts, and fell before the throne on their faces, and worshipped God,

7:12 Saying, Amen: Blessing, and glory, and wisdom, and thanksgiving, and honour, and power, and might, be unto our God for ever and ever. Amen.

7:13 And one of the elders answered, saying unto me, What are these which are arrayed in white robes? and whence came they?

7:14 And I said unto him, Sir, thou knowest. And he said to me, These are they which came out of great tribulation, and have washed their robes, and made them white in the blood of the Lamb.

7:15 Therefore are they before the throne of God, and serve him day and night in his temple: and he that sitteth on the throne shall dwell among them.

7:16 They shall hunger no more, neither thirst any more; neither shall the sun light on them, nor any heat.

7:17 For the Lamb in the midst of the throne shall feed them, and shall lead them unto living fountains of waters: and God shall wipe away all tears from their eyes.

In this vision, John hears an elder from one tribe of Israel asking, *Who are these arrayed in white robes, and where did they come from?*. Clearly the elder was not prepared for what was before him. Paul in his letter to the Ephesians reveals what many Jews find hard to understand:

> *For this cause I Paul, the prisoner of Jesus Christ for you Gentiles, If ye have heard of the dispensation of the grace of God which is given me to you-ward: How that by revelation he made known unto me the mystery; (as I wrote afore in few words, Whereby, when ye read, ye may understand my knowledge in the mystery of Christ) Which in other ages was not made known unto the sons of men, as it is now revealed unto his holy Apostles and prophets by the Spirit; That the Gentiles should be fellowheirs, and of the same body, and partakers of his promise in Christ by the Gospel: Whereof I was made a minister, according to the gift of the grace of God given unto me by the effectual working of his power* (Ephesians 3:1-7).

Evidently the elder at first had difficulty understanding how one could attain righteousness without the law. Here we observe that both Jews and Gentiles are full of praise because of the realisation they belong to Christ forevermore. They are nourished by the Word, refreshed by the Spirit and therefore will never again succumb to doubt. They realise that what they had always hungered and thirsted for was found in 'the wisdom of the knowledge and revelation of Christ' (Ephesians 1:17). The elder here reminds us of why humanity should celebrate the gift of God's grace. It is understandable why the elder wondered who the strangers were and where they had come from. For a Gentile to be invited into the very presence of God simply by 'faith alone' rather than through 'the keeping of the law' was once unthinkable for an elder of Israel.

REVELATION 8

8:1 And when he had opened the seventh seal, there was silence in heaven about the space of half an hour.

8:2 And I saw the seven angels which stood before God; and to them were given seven trumpets.

8:3 And another angel came and stood at the altar, having a golden censer; and there was given unto him much incense, that he should offer it with the prayers of all saints upon the golden altar which was before the throne.

8:4 And the smoke of the incense, which came with the prayers of the saints, ascended up before God out of the angel's hand.

8:5 And the angel took the censer, and filled it with fire of the altar, and cast it into the earth: and there were voices, and thunderings, and lightnings, and an earthquake.

8:6 And the seven angels which had the seven trumpets prepared themselves to sound.

The 'thunderings, lightnings and earthquake' draw our attention to 'the end of all things'. Jesus' entry into Jerusalem was first heralded with the song 'Hosanna to the son of David', followed by his trial, judgment, and crucifixion, symbolised here as a 'censer' being filled with fire and thrown to the earth. The 'silence in heaven for half an hour' represents Jesus' final hours. The seven angels were given seven trumpets to herald the beginning of events that were to end with the final judgment of Jerusalem. The 'other angel' with the golden censer and given much incense can be none other than the Apostle Paul. Paul was the most prolific New Testament writer that has given us a much broader insight into our understanding and meaning of Christ.

8:7 The first angel sounded, and there followed hail and fire mingled with blood, and they were cast upon the earth: and the third part of trees was burnt up, and all green grass was burnt up.

8:8 And the second angel sounded, and as it were a great mountain burning with fire was cast into the sea: and the third part of the sea became blood;

8:9 And the third part of the creatures which were in the sea, and had life, died; and the third part of the ships were destroyed.

While the symbolism of destructive forces such as hail and fire mingled with blood may imply death and destruction, there is a positive lesson here regarding 'life in the spirit'. Each of the seven Epistles, whether written by Paul, Peter, James, John, Timothy, Titus, or Jude, each Epistle remind us that God's kingdom is spiritual and permanent and will never be broken. The 'second angel' draws our attention to what the Old Testament prophet Daniel had described as a stone that was 'cut from a mountain without hands and dashed all earthly kingdoms to pieces', signifying the time when Christ was to set up a kingdom on earth that could never be broken (Daniel 2:34, 35).

Notice that while the creatures of the sea die and a third of the ships perish, the Kingdom of God remains. Although many battles have been fought on land and sea, and much blood spilled, all efforts for peace through war have failed and always will. The 'great mountain' that was thrown into the sea marked the end of a religion that was based on law.

8:10 And the third angel sounded, and there fell a great star from heaven, burning as it were a lamp, and it fell upon the third part of the rivers, and upon the fountains of waters;

8:11 And the name of the star is called Wormwood: and the third part of the waters became wormwood; and many men died of the waters, because they were made bitter.

The 'star' here is figurative of Jesus 'teachings of justice an mercy'. To the religious leaders of the day, his words were as bitter as wormwood to those who opposed him. But not all who heard the teachings of Jesus found his words to be bitter. For example, when Jesus met a Samaritan woman drawing water from a well, he explained to her that should she drink the water from the true fountain of life she would never thirst again. Although Samaritans were at variance with the Jews, she realised 'the worship of God in spirit and in truth' is what 'quenching the thirst' truly means (John 4:526). Unlike the Scribes and Pharisees who found Jesus' words to be bitter, the Samaritan woman found his words to be sweet.

8:12 And the fourth angel sounded, and the third part of the sun was smitten, and the third part of the moon, and the third part of the stars; so as the third part of them was darkened, and the day shone not for a third part of it, and the night likewise.

8:13 And I beheld, and heard an angel flying through the midst of heaven, saying with a loud voice, Woe, woe, woe, to the inhabiters of the earth by reason of the other voices of the trumpet of the three angels, which are yet to sound!

The sun, moon and stars are merely shadows of the true light of Christ. On the day of the crucifixion, Matthew, Mark and Luke recorded the time when darkness overshadowed the land of Judea. It was a dark day for those who believed in Jesus. Whether one believes it was literal darkness or simply an expression used for those who had lost hope when Jesus was crucified, it was a dark day for those who had expectations of a king to free Israel from the yoke of Rome.

> *Now from the sixth hour until the ninth hour there was darkness over the land* (Matthew 27:45; Mark 15:33; Luke 23:44).

REVELATION 9

9:1 And the fifth angel sounded, and I saw a star fall from heaven unto the earth: and to him was given the key of the bottomless pit.

9:2 And he opened the bottomless pit; and there arose a smoke out of the pit, as the smoke of a great furnace; and the sun and the air were darkened by reason of the smoke of the pit.

The battle between the dark forces and the light of Christ was soon to be revealed within the hearts and minds of all nations, tongues, and people, beginning at Jerusalem and the regions of Judea. This battle could only be fought and won by the One holding the key of David. Redemption is now offered to those who have, since the beginning of the world, died without hope. In the words of Ezekiel,

> *When I shall bring thee down with them that descend into the pit, with the people of old time, and shall set thee in the low parts of the earth, in places desolate of old, with them that go down to the pit, that thou be not inhabited; and I shall set glory in the land of the living* (Ezekiel 26:20).

And in the words of David,

> *The heathen are sunk down in the pit that they made: in the net which they hid is their own foot taken* (Psalm 9:15).

Jesus' sole purpose was to set free all who were captive and bound by the things of this world:

> *The Spirit of the Lord is upon me, because he hath anointed me to preach the Gospel to the poor; he hath sent me to heal the brokenhearted, to preach deliverance to the captives, and recovering of sight to the blind, to set at liberty them that are bruised, To preach the acceptable year of the Lord* (Luke 4:18-19).

John now sees in his vision Jesus Christ preparing for battle against the dark forces of this world. He does not go to battle with a physical sword, shedding blood as David had when defeating his enemies, but sheds his own blood while accompanied by the power and Spirit of his words:

> *For the word of God is quick, and powerful, and sharper than any twoedged sword, piercing even to the dividing asunder of soul and spirit, and of the joints and marrow, and is a discerner of the thoughts and intents of the heart* (Hebrews 4:12).

> *For we wrestle not against flesh and blood, but against principalities, against powers, against the rulers of the darkness of this world, against spiritual wickedness in high places* (Ephesians 6:12).

Paul's reference above refers to the religious powers that established their authority in his day, and continue to this day, in concealing the knowledge of Christ. Those who plotted against Jesus were from amongst his own people, especially the leaders of the synagogues who were friends of Herod. The Jewish leaders had resisted the teachings of Jesus since they consciously knew of the corruption being exposed. John the Baptist had been put to death because he spoke openly about the moral corruption within Herod's family. Rather than have their hearts and minds opened to Jesus' teaching about the Kingdom of God, the Jewish leaders and political powers kept up their resistance. While many of the common people heard Jesus gladly, the religious leaders took every opportunity to find fault with his teaching.

Although many understood Jesus' parables, many remained within their own 'prison house of sin'. The bottomless pit is figurative for those who remain in darkness. Meanwhile the one who holds the key has the authority and power to bring light to those in darkness so the spirit may be set free from the bondage of religion.

9:3   And there came out of the smoke locusts upon the earth: and unto them was given power, as the scorpions of the earth have power.

9:4   And it was commanded them that they should not hurt the grass of the earth, neither any green thing, neither any tree; but only those men which have not the seal of God in their foreheads.

9:5   And to them it was given that they should not kill them, but that they should be tormented five months: and their torment was as the torment of a scorpion, when he striketh a man.

As noticed in Revelation 8:7, the Creator alone has the power to *'harm the grass, any green thing, or tree'*. Locusts in the Old Testament are characterised as instruments of God that devour plant life, and characterized as a warning by calling people to repentance to preserve their lives.

> *Else, if thou refuse to let my people go, behold, tomorrow will I bring the locusts into thy coast* (Exodus 10:4).

The locusts have the potential to kill or harm although they are restrained from doing so. For 'five months' they are given the authority to torment all who do not have the seal of God on their foreheads. The only other mention that corresponds with 'five months' is found in Genesis 7:24 where the waters had prevailed on the earth for one hundred and fifty days, which in ancient Jewish reckoning represented five lots of thirty days, or five months. Water symbolises the saving of souls and a believer's willingness to be 'dead to sin' by being symbolically buried and resurrected to a new creation in Christ. However, rather than perish with the flood of untruths that prevailed in Jesus' time, the religious leaders continued to resist his teachings. In a later chapter we are shown the extent of what the enemy of the true church was prepared to do:

> *"And the serpent cast out of his mouth water as a flood after the woman, that he may cause her to be carried away of the flood* (Revelation 12:15).

This chapter reveals how the words of Jesus, like those in the days of Noah, were a torment only to those who opposed the teachings about the Kingdom of God. Here the locust is symbolic of how the Word of God eats everything within its path:

> *But what saith it? The word is nigh thee, even in thy mouth, and in thy heart: that is, the word of faith, which we preach* (Romans 10:8).

Matthew's gospel gives an example of two tormented souls:

> *And, behold, they cried out, saying, What have we to do with thee, Jesus, thou Son of God? art thou come hither to torment us before the time?* (Matthew 8:29).

9:6 And in those days shall men seek death, and shall not find it; and shall desire to die, and death shall flee from them.

Seeking death to escape the penalty of sin, or responsibility of any wrongs, is not within humanity's power. We cannot escape a self fulfilling judgment that results from our conduct and behaviour within this life. It is understandable why many take their own lives because of unfortunate circumstances, but to take one's own life to escape the responsibility for the evil committed is not that simple. The power over life and death is not given to men, but to Christ.

9:7 And the shapes of the locusts were like unto horses prepared unto battle; and on their heads were as it were crowns like gold, and their faces were as the faces of men.

9:8   And they had hair as the hair of women, and their teeth were as the teeth of lions.

9:9   And they had breastplates, as it were breastplates of iron; and the sound of their wings was as the sound of chariots of many horses running to battle.

9:10 And they had tails like unto scorpions, and there were stings in their tails: and their power was to hurt men five months.

John's Revelation reveals much about the Word of God in which everything else pales into insignificance. Consider the following:

- The Word of God is more precious than gold

- The Word of God may be proclaimed by men and women.

- The Word of God has power as the teeth of a lion.

- The Word of God protects as a breastplate of iron.

- The Word of God resounds around the world.

- The Word of God can sting like nothing else.

- The Word of God was rejected in Noah's day (here symbolised by the five months during which water covered the earth).

9:11 And they had a king over them, which is the angel of the bottomless pit, whose name in the Hebrew tongue is Abaddon, but in the Greek tongue hath his name Apollyon.

9:12 One woe is past; and, behold, there come two woes more hereafter.

The Apostle Paul's influence in teaching Christ and spreading the good news of the gospel cannot be overstated. Jesus and the disciples, along with Paul and the Apostles, played two roles.

Although Abaddon is understood traditionally in Hebrew as the messenger of death, here we observe Abaddon in the Greek translation as Apollyon. Both Abaddon and Apollyon represent 'death', in this case, Paul and the Apostles are described as Apollyon, as messengers of 'death to law'. With this background John sees those singing 'the song of Moses' which represented 'law', and 'the song of the Lamb' which now represents the gospel.

It is interesting to note the mention of the 'first woe' in this section. Jesus spoke of 'woes' describing those who have only an outward appearance of Christ, namely the Scribes, Pharisees, described by Jesus as Hypocrites. The woes reveal the true nature of those who were opposed to Jesus teaching and the continued teaching of the Apostles. Here again the woes remind us of the hypocrisy of those who believe in keeping the law to earn favour with God. Jesus' woes from Mathew's gospel show striking parallels with Paul's messages to the seven churches. Each woe focuses on those teachers of the law who use religion rather than Christ as a means of righteousness:

> *But woe unto you, Scribes and Pharisees, hypocrites! for ye shut up the kingdom of heaven against men: for ye neither go in yourselves, neither suffer ye them that are entering to go in.*
>
> *Woe unto you, Scribes and Pharisees, hypocrites! for ye devour widows' houses, and for a pretence make long prayer: therefore ye shall receive the greater damnation.*
>
> *Woe unto you, Scribes and Pharisees, hypocrites! for ye compass sea and land to make one proselyte, and when he is made, ye make him twofold more the child of hell than yourselves.*
>
> *Woe unto you, ye blind guides, which say, Whosoever shall swear by the temple, it is nothing; but whosoever shall swear by the gold of the temple, he is a debtor! Ye fools and blind: for whether is greater, the gold, or the temple that sanctifieth the gold? And, Whosoever shall swear by the altar, it is nothing; but whosoever sweareth by the gift that is upon it, he is guilty. Ye fools and blind: for whether is greater, the gift, or the altar that sanctifieth the gift? Whoso therefore shall swear by the*

altar, sweareth by it, and by all things thereon. And whoso shall swear by the temple, sweareth by it, and by him that dwelleth therein. And he that shall swear by heaven, sweareth by the throne of God, and by him that sitteth thereon.

Woe unto you, Scribes and Pharisees, hypocrites! for ye pay tithe of mint and anise and cummin, and have omitted the weightier matters of the law, judgment, mercy, and faith: these ought ye to have done, and not to leave the other undone. Ye blind guides, which strain at a gnat, and swallow a camel.

Woe unto you, Scribes and Pharisees, hypocrites! for ye make clean the outside of the cup and of the platter, but within they are full of extortion and excess. Thou blind Pharisee, cleanse first that which is within the cup and platter, that the outside of them may be clean also.

Woe unto you, Scribes and Pharisees, hypocrites! for ye are like unto whited sepulchres, which indeed appear beautiful outward, but are within full of dead men's bones, and of all uncleanness. Even so ye also outwardly appear righteous unto men, but within ye are full of hypocrisy and iniquity.

Woe unto you, Scribes and Pharisees, hypocrites! because ye build the tombs of the prophets, and garnish the sepulchres of the righteous (Matthew 23:13-29).

The woes speak for themselves. The hypocrisy within the religion of Judaism is typical of all religions invented by men. Every religion within every nation has rules and regulations of behaviour, yet none can say that what they teach can permanently change the heart. The woes describe the futility of religion grounded in law. The 'faith of Jesus' is not a religion, but an individual awakening from spiritual slumber.

9:13   And the sixth angel sounded, and I heard a voice from the four horns of the golden altar which is before God,

9:14   Saying to the sixth angel which had the trumpet, Loose the four angels which are bound in the great river Euphrates.

9:15 And the four angels were loosed, which were prepared for an hour, and a day, and a month, and a year, for to slay the third part of men.

9:16 And the number of the army of the horsemen were two hundred thousand thousand: and I heard the number of them.

9:17 And thus I saw the horses in the vision, and them that sat on them, having breastplates of fire, and of jacinth, and brimstone: and the heads of the horses were as the heads of lions; and out of their mouths issued fire and smoke and brimstone.

9:18 By these three was the third part of men killed, by the fire, and by the smoke, and by the brimstone, which issued out of their mouths.

9:19 For their power is in their mouth, and in their tails: for their tails were like unto serpents, and had heads, and with them they do hurt.

9:20 And the rest of the men which were not killed by these plagues yet repented not of the works of their hands, that they should not worship devils, and idols of gold, and silver, and brass, and stone, and of wood: which neither can see, nor hear, nor walk:

9:21 Neither repented they of their murders, nor of their sorceries, nor of their fornication, nor of their thefts.

David had extended his empire to the borders of the great river Euphrates, the location of many fierce battles of which he won. The above verses reveal the time that the final great battle had begun. Although David's physical kingdom was glorious, it was earthly and temporal. Now it was time to symbolically cross the great river Euphrates which a thousand years earlier was a barrier to the expansion of David's earthly kingdom. It was now time for

Jesus, 'the Root and Offspring of David' to gather his followers and extend the borders of what was a temporal earthly kingdom into a permanent and spiritual kingdom.

The Word of God is here symbolised as fire, smoke, and brimstone because of the effect that the power of the Gospel of Christ has over humanity whether or not one has even heard of the gospel. Paul used a similar expression of fire when quoting from the Old Testament book of Proverbs.

> *Therefore if thine enemy hunger, feed him; if he thirst, give him drink: for in so doing thou shalt heap coals of fire on his head* (Romans 12:20).

To the Pharisees, Jesus' message was as though fire, smoke, and brimstone had descended on them. His three and a half years of teaching the word, followed by the Apostle's three and a half years preaching to the Jews which culminated in the stoning of Steven, paved the way for the gospel to be preached beyond the borders of Judea.

Revelation 10

10:1 And I saw another mighty angel come down from heaven, clothed with a cloud: and a rainbow was upon his head, and his face was as it were the sun, and his feet as pillars of fire:

10:2 And he had in his hand a little book open: and he set his right foot upon the sea, and his left foot on the earth,

10:3 And cried with a loud voice, as when a lion roareth: and when he had cried, seven thunders uttered their voices.

10:4 And when the seven thunders had uttered their voices, I was about to write: and I heard a voice from heaven saying unto me, Seal up those things which the seven thunders uttered, and write them not.

10:5 And the angel which I saw stand upon the sea and upon the earth lifted up his hand to heaven,

10:6 And sware by him that liveth for ever and ever, who created heaven, and the things that therein are, and the earth, and the things that therein are, and the sea, and the things which are therein, that there should be time no longer:

10:7 But in the days of the voice of the seventh angel, when he shall begin to sound, the mystery of God should be finished, as he hath declared to his servants the prophets.

In this chapter, John's vision regarding the tribulations and trials of the early church has reached the halfway mark. The messenger is here depicted as a 'mighty angel' no doubt holding a book with a message addressed to Israel (Romans 1:16). This book takes precedence over the books of the 'law and the prophets' symbolised by the 'pillar of fire', a reminder of Israel's wilderness journeys when they were led by a pillar of fire while living by the laws of Moses.

The Gospel of Christ was now revealed through Apollyon, symbolised here by the seven thunders which represent the spirit and magnitude of the Word revealed within the Apostle's letters that brings death to the law. The stoning of Stephen signalled a final rejection by the Jews because the gospel message was not welcomed in Jerusalem. This chapter reveals the turning point in history that marked the message of Apollyon to the 'Jew first' and to the Gentile world (Romans 1:16).

10:8 And the voice which I heard from heaven spake unto me again, and said, Go and take the little book which is open in the hand of the angel which standeth upon the sea and upon the earth.

10:9 And I went unto the angel, and said unto him, Give me the little book. And he said unto me, Take it, and eat it up; and it shall make thy belly bitter, but it shall be in thy mouth sweet as honey.

10:10 And I took the little book out of the angel's hand, and ate it up; and it was in my mouth sweet as honey: and as soon as I had eaten it, my belly was bitter.

10:11 And he said unto me, Thou must prophesy again before many peoples, and nations, and tongues, and kings.

One of the most powerful testimonies of faith recorded in the New Testament is the account of the conversion of Saul, renamed Paul, on meeting Jesus on the road to Damascus. Paul called himself a

Pharisee of Pharisees, an exceptional scholar in all things relating to the law and the prophets. Paul's realisation that he was chosen by Jesus to preach the gospel was both sweet and bitter (Ephesians 1:4, 5). His closely held beliefs regarding the law were challenged once he had met Jesus and experienced a 'revelation' of Jesus Christ. Paul soon realised that preaching Christ would be something the Jews would not find easy to digest. When he embraced the faith of Jesus he was compelled to teach others a better way, not preaching 'to' people, nations, tongues, and kings, but 'about' peoples, nations, tongues, and kings. Paul knew that he had a message about the destiny of humanity and the election of grace and therefore he was compelled to share the gospel with the world.

REVELATION 11

11:1   And there was given me a reed like unto a rod: and the angel stood, saying, Rise, and measure the temple of God, and the altar, and them that worship therein.

11:2   But the court which is without the temple leave out, and measure it not; for it is given unto the Gentiles: and the holy city shall they tread under foot forty and two months.

Long before the body of Christ and temple of God was functioning as the 'church', Moses was commanded to set up a temporary earthly tabernacle administered by earthly priests who could only symbolically cleanse the soul. Once a year the earthly priest sprinkled the blood of bulls and goats upon the mercy seat, signifying the remission of sins under the law. However, when Jesus offered his body by the shedding of his own blood, he became a high priest of a better covenant. The veil that represented the conflict between the flesh and the spirit was torn in two when Jesus uttered 'it is finished'.

The measuring rod depicts those who had worshipped in spirit and in truth. The forty-two months denote the time during which the worshippers of the earthly tabernacle rejected the message of Jesus. The Pharisees had to 'tread the holy city underfoot' in their eagerness to kill Jesus for fear of an uprising if they pursued him openly. It may appear that the Gentiles are those who tread the holy city underfoot since the assumption may be that 'they' refers to the Gentiles. However, it was the religious leaders of the nation of

Israel and those who worshipped the idols of stone, gold and wood within the temple, who were the real enemies of Jesus. The forty-two months is used only once again and refers to the dragon that gives the beast its power to those who are the real enemies of Christ (Revelation 13:5).

This chapter intentionally shows the shift from Judaism to the Gentile world because of Israel's rejection of Jesus Christ. The deliberate rejection of the teachings of Jesus opened the door for the gathering of the nations of the world to worship in spirit and in truth; hence the measuring rod (Romans 10, 11).

There is much debate about the 'three and a half years, forty-two months, one thousand and sixty days, and 'time, times, and dividing of times'. For example, Daniel refers only twice to 'time, times, and dividing of times'. Many biblical scholars have assumed that John's visions of 'forty-two months' and 'three and a half years' (which equate to one thousand, two hundred and sixty days) are linked to the same time. However, while those various descriptions of time may appear to be related, Daniel does not mention 'three and a half years', 'forty-two months', or 'one thousand, two hundred and sixty days'.

The three and a half years relate to the messages and work of Christ Jesus, the forty-two months to the enemies of Jesus during his ministry, and the one thousand, two hundred and sixty days, the setting up of the church. Daniel's mention of 'time, times, and dividing of times' encompasses everything from Daniel's time to the time of Jesus that had finally revealed the completeness of the work of Christ, including the consummation at the 'end of time' in 70 A.D. Paul's first letter to Ephesus sums up both Daniel's prophecies and the fulfilment of the finished work of Christ (Ephesians 3:1-21).

11:3   And I will give power unto my two witnesses, and they shall prophesy a thousand two hundred and threescore days, clothed in sackcloth.

11:4   These are the two olive trees, and the two candlesticks standing before the God of the earth.

11:5 And if any man will hurt them, fire proceedeth out of their mouth, and devoureth their enemies: and if any man will hurt them, he must in this manner be killed.

11:6 These have power to shut heaven, that it rain not in the days of their prophecy: and have power over waters to turn them to blood, and to smite the earth with all plagues, as often as they will.

The one thousand, two hundred and sixty days, is the same period as forty two months, and three and half years of time. Those times relate to Jesus ministry and establishment of the church and the opposition encountered while establishing the church of the firstborn.

Moses and Elijah were the figures of the two witnesses. A vision of Elijah was necessary to show 'the spirit of Elijah' that is necessary to withstand the threat of persecution (Matthew 17:2,3).

The olive trees and candlesticks are here symbolized by the Spirit and Word that had witnessed the marriage of Christ and the church, 'the bride of Christ'. The Spirit and Word are the olive trees and lamps that represent the light of the gospel preached to the Jews during Jesus one thousand two hundred and sixty days of ministry. The Spirit and Word are the witnesses to Christ and the church that had become one flesh through marriage (Ephesians 5:31-32).

The appearance of Moses and Elijah on the Mount of Transfiguration was to reveal the finished work of the Spirit and Word. Moses was handed the law engraved in stone that typified the hardness of the hearts of many Jews, while Elijah was a man of faith through whom the power of prayer opened and shut the heavens with a drought for three and a half years followed by rain for three and a half years.

11:7 And when they shall have finished their testimony, the beast that ascendeth out of the bottomless pit shall make war against them, and shall overcome them, and kill them.

> **11:8** And their dead bodies shall lie in the street of the great city, which spiritually is called Sodom and Egypt, where also our Lord was crucified.

The secular and religious powers of the day were always on guard, fearing an uprising that could weaken their position and control. It was therefore necessary for John to reveal his visions in symbols for the church's protection. Here we notice a 'beast' ascending from the bottomless pit. This beastly power was asleep and undisturbed until Jesus began his preaching. Although Jesus was critical of the religious leaders under the strict rules of the Sanhedrin, he was mindful that they had the power to silence him. This figurative beast had no option but to come out of the pit and plot the death of Jesus who by now had reached the legal age necessary to preach in the synagogues. His claim to have authority to forgive sins incited the beastly powers to bring a charge of blasphemy against him.

Jesus' words were a testimony to the Spirit and power of the Word. His teachings had disturbed the religious leaders to where they had no option but to plot his death. The Spirit and Word may have appeared to be dead when Jesus hung on the cross, but forty years later, Jerusalem, here figuratively called Sodom and Egypt, witnessed how the Spirit and Word that had prophesied the day of judgment against Israel, was alive. The Spirit and Word had finished their testimony about the fate of Jerusalem, and remains alive within Christ and the church to this day.

> **11:9** And they of the people and kindreds and tongues and nations shall see their dead bodies three days and an half, and shall not suffer their dead bodies to be put in graves.
>
> **11:10** And they that dwell upon the earth shall rejoice over them, and make merry, and shall send gifts one to another; because these two prophets tormented them that dwelt on the earth.

Notice the two distinct and separate camps. There are those from the tribes, tongues, nations, represented by those who were 'heavenly minded' such as Joseph of Arimathea who requested that the body of Jesus should be taken from the place of crucifixion before his legs were broken and his remains thrown into a common grave. There were also the Scribes, Pharisees, and unbelievers who 'dwell on the earth', who rejoiced that Jesus would be silenced forever. Those who celebrated the death of Jesus had little regard for the poor, the hungry, the sick, and those oppressed by the lack of compassion of the religious leaders of the day.

11:11   And after three days and an half the spirit of life from God entered into them, and they stood upon their feet; and great fear fell upon them which saw them.

11:12   And they heard a great voice from heaven saying unto them, Come up hither. And they ascended up to heaven in a cloud; and their enemies beheld them.

11:13   And the same hour was there a great earthquake, and the tenth part of the city fell, and in the earthquake were slain of men seven thousand: and the remnant were affrighted, and gave glory to the God of heaven.

11:14   The second woe is past; and, behold, the third woe cometh quickly.

The 'three and a half days' denote the prophetic time of Jesus' three and a half year ministry. Some scholars suggest that Wednesday rather than a Friday was the day of crucifixion, therefore from midday Wednesday to sunset the following Saturday, was three and a half days. While there may be some merit in that conclusion, the day for a year principle regarding Jesus three and a half year ministry is more likely.

Since the crucifixion and subsequent appearance to his disciples on the road to Damascus, Jesus then spent forty days meeting with his disciples and speaking about things pertaining to the Kingdom of

God (Acts 1:3). Ten days later, the Holy Spirit descended on the day of Pentecost from where the Holy Spirit became active amongst the disciples and the congregation. It was likened to an 'earthquake', since it had shaken those that were formally enemies of Jesus. The 'seven thousand' is figurative of those who scoffed at Peter's preaching when speaking of the prophet Joel's promise about the day that the Holy Spirit would be given to all who would call on God (Acts 2:13. 2:16-21).

The remnant was frightened because the presence and power of the Holy Spirit was something never witnessed. Once the noise of what was described as 'a rushing mighty wind' had subsided, the believers gave glory to their God (Acts 2:46). The experience at Pentecost was very different to what the disciples had experienced after the crucifixion. They were disappointed because they expected that a new and glorious Israel would be restored by a fearless warrior like David who hopefully had the military might to overcome the Roman occupation through physical force. While their expectations were dashed when Jesus was crucified, their disappointment turned to joy when Jesus approached them on the road to Damascus and explained everything about himself, beginning with the Old Testament prophecies about his ministry and crucifixion.

> *Then he said unto them, O fools, and slow of heart to believe all that the prophets have spoken: Ought not Christ to have suffered these things, and to enter into his glory? And beginning at Moses and all the prophets, he expounded unto them in all the scriptures the things concerning himself* (Luke 24:25-27).

The disciples came to understand the true meaning of Daniel's prophecies about Christ Jesus' victory in overcoming the world and setting up a kingdom that would never be destroyed. Pentecost marked the beginning of the infant church's rapid growth.

11:15 And the seventh angel sounded; and there were great voices in heaven, saying, The kingdoms of this world are become the kingdoms of our Lord, and of his Christ; and he shall reign for ever and ever.

11:16 And the four and twenty elders, which sat before God on their seats, fell upon their faces, and worshipped God,

11:17 Saying, We give thee thanks, O Lord God Almighty, which art, and wast, and art to come; because thou hast taken to thee thy great power, and hast reigned.

11:18 And the nations were angry, and thy wrath is come, and the time of the dead, that they should be judged, and that thou shouldest give reward unto thy servants the prophets, and to the saints, and them that fear thy name, small and great; and shouldest destroy them which destroy the earth.

11:19 And the temple of God was opened in heaven, and there was seen in his temple the ark of his testament: and there were lightnings, and voices, and thunderings, and an earthquake, and great hail.

Many elders amongst the remnant of Israel had by now acknowledged that Jesus Christ was the anointed one that had accomplished God's will. The Ark of the Covenant was a reminder that everything the law required had now been fulfilled in Jesus Christ. The lightning, noise, thundering and earthquakes resonated with the power of God's grace given to all. The law was fulfilled and had no power to condemn those who were now in Christ and walking in the spirit. The 'great hail' is a reminder of those who had persecuted and rejected Jesus, symbolized here by the way they had turned 'the water of life' into hail that typified the hardness and coldness of their hearts.

REVELATION 12

12:1 And there appeared a great wonder in heaven; a woman clothed with the sun, and the moon under her feet, and upon her head a crown of twelve stars:

12:2 And she being with child cried, travailing in birth, and pained to be delivered.

Paul's letter to the Galatians reveals an interesting analogy of law and grace by introducing the story of two women with a profound influence on the destiny of the Arabs and Jews. In the comparison between Sarah and Agar (Hagar), Paul attempted to teach the Jews the difference between law and grace:

> *Tell me, ye that desire to be under the law, do ye not hear the law? For it is written, that Abraham had two sons, the one by a bondmaid, the other by a freewoman. But he who was of the bondwoman was born after the flesh; but he of the freewoman was by promise. Which things are an allegory: for these are the two covenants; the one from the mount Sinai, which gendereth to bondage, which is Agar. For this Agar is mount Sinai in Arabia, and answereth to Jerusalem which now is, and is in bondage with her children. But Jerusalem which is above is free, which is the mother of us all. For it is written, Rejoice, thou barren that bearest not; break forth and cry, thou that travailest not: for the desolate hath many more children than she which hath an husband. Now we, brethren, as Isaac was, are the children of promise. But as then he that was born after the flesh persecuted*

him that was born after the Spirit, even so it is now. Nevertheless what saith the scripture? Cast out the bondwoman and her son: for the son of the bondwoman shall not be heir with the son of the freewoman. So then, brethren, we are not children of the bondwoman, but of the free (Galatians 4: 21-31).

Through the womb of Sarah, twelve tribes were born, one of which would give birth to a child that would bring light to the world. The offspring of the woman was the infant church that was to go through 'the great tribulation' before triumphing over its enemies. The time between Jesus' crucifixion and 70 A.D. saw a time of fierce opposition against the infant church, hence the travailing and pain in delivery. On the other hand, Hagar also gave birth to the father of a nation that would govern by law rather than grace. One woman represented grace, the other represented law. Pentecost saw the beginning of the 'labour pains' that the church was about to endure. The twelve stars signify the light of the twelve Apostles, while the moon that reflects the light from the sun and stars represents the church that first carried the gospel light into the known world. The 'crying out' characterises the prayers and suffering that the early church endured before it won the victory over the enemy.

12:3   And there appeared another wonder in heaven; and behold a great red dragon, having seven heads and ten horns, and seven crowns upon his heads.

12:4   And his tail drew the third part of the stars of heaven, and did cast them to the earth: and the dragon stood before the woman which was ready to be delivered, for to devour her child as soon as it was born.

12:5   And she brought forth a man child, who was to rule all nations with a rod of iron: and her child was caught up unto God, and to his throne.

12:6   And the woman fled into the wilderness, where she hath a place prepared of God, that they should feed her there a thousand two hundred and threescore days.

The dragon with seven heads and ten horns and seven crowns is the figurative union of secular and religious powers, past, present and future. The stars that are swept out of the sky and flung to earth represent those who were about to be tortured and killed by the religious and secular powers that persecuted the infant church. Jesus had warned that many would betray one another because of the persecution to follow[3].

Paul wrote expressly 'to the Jew first' hoping to convince the nation of Israel that 'the faith of Jesus' would overcome the world and every obstacle put before them (Revelation 14:12). Paul's uncompromising knowledge of Christ and his knowledge of the laws and customs of the Jews helped establish the church to rule with a 'rod of iron'. Although the infant church won the victory by demonstrating how faith works by love rather than by the deeds of the law, it was not without casualties. The battle lines were drawn between law and grace. For instance, when Peter compromised his position by joining in with the Jewish custom of not sharing a meal with Gentiles, Paul rebuked him because there could be no middle ground.

> *But when Peter was come to Antioch, I withstood him to the face, because he was to be blamed. For before that certain came from James, he did eat with the Gentiles: but when they were come, he withdrew and separated himself, fearing them which were of the circumcision. And the other Jews dissembled likewise with him; insomuch that Barnabas also was carried away with their dissimulation. But when I saw that they walked not uprightly according to the truth of the Gospel, I said unto Peter before them all, If thou, being a Jew, livest after the manner of Gentiles, and not as do the Jews, why compellest thou the Gentiles to live as do the Jews? We who are Jews by nature, and not sinners of the Gentiles, Knowing that a man is not justified by the works of the law, but by the faith of Jesus Christ, even we have believed in Jesus Christ, that we might be justified by the faith of Christ, and not by the works of the law: for by the works of the law shall no flesh be justified. But*

---

3 (See commentary on Mathew 24).

if, while we seek to be justified by Christ, we ourselves also are found sinners, is therefore Christ the minister of sin? God forbid. For if I build again the things which I destroyed, I make myself a transgressor. For I through the law am dead to the law, that I might live unto God. I am crucified with Christ: nevertheless I live; yet not I, but Christ liveth in me: and the life which I now live in the flesh I live by the faith of the Son of God, who loved me, and gave himself for me. I do not frustrate the grace of God: for if righteousness come by the law, then Christ is dead in vain (Galatians 2:11-21).

This was just one example of Paul's frustrations trying to persuade the Jews that neither circumcision nor keeping the laws of Moses could save sinners. Contrary to what secular and religious powers may one day enforce as a guide for moral standards, the gospels could not be clearer in explaining the true nature of those who are now in Christ. History proves that teaching the Ten Commandments as a moral standard does not fix the moral problems of society. The religions of Judaism and Islam that sprang from the wombs of Sarah and Hagar remain to this day divided by hatred simply because the law cannot change the heart. Unfortunately, Christianity as it stands today, is no longer capable of teaching how the knowledge of Christ can bring Israel and the Arab nations together as one faith.

In this chapter we are reminded of the powers at work that keep humanity bound by fear. Rome knew that keeping the peace with Israel was in the best interests of both parties. The ten horns of the dragon are symbolic of those empires throughout history which have divided and conquered by setting up smaller powers as instruments that serve the higher powers in enforcing law. The later emergence of the 'Church of Rome' as the official state religion under Constantine was 'the falling away' that had already begun in Paul's day. Although having only the outward appearance of Christ, this union with Judaic law had set the stage for the Antichrist to set up its own priesthood and worship of an external son of god.

This chapter speaks about the powers at work trying to silence the early church. From the middle of the first century until the early fourth century, Antichrist was being set up as the official state religion that falsely claims to represent Christ to this day. The Nicene Creed, which is accepted by almost the entire world of Christendom as a statement of belief had omitted the most important teaching of the New Testament regarding the substance and nature of Christ. From the beginning of the second century until the early fourth century there was much debate about the nature of the Father, Son, and the Holy Spirit. The term 'trinity' was invented to dispel any doubt that 'Jesus is God'. Certain bishops were resolute in their belief there was to be only one true Catholic Church, and outside of which there could be no salvation. The bishops further decreed that any teachings outside the universal Catholic Church would be condemned as heresy. At the end of the third century and the beginning of the fourth, heretics who disagreed with the church's fundamental beliefs were expelled or murdered. A creed came into existence to end all arguments about the nature of 'Jesus'. The creed was the final word on ecclesiastical issues that remain to this day the foundational teaching on the nature of Jesus. The creed formed in 325 A.D, which was later ratified to include the trinity doctrine that reads:

> *We believe in one God, the Father, the Almighty, maker of heaven and earth, of all that is, seen and unseen. We believe in one Lord, Jesus Christ, the only Son of God, eternally begotten of the Father, God from God, Light from Light, true God from true God, begotten, not made, of one Being with the Father. Through him all things were made. For us and for our salvation he came down from heaven: by the power of the Holy Spirit he became incarnate from the Virgin Mary, and was made man. For our sake he was crucified under Pontius Pilate; he suffered death and was buried. On the third day he rose again in accordance with the Scriptures; he ascended into heaven and is seated at the right hand of the Father. He will come again in glory to judge the living and the dead, and his kingdom will have no end. We believe in the Holy Spirit, the Lord, the giver of life, who proceeds from the Father and the Son. With the Father and the Son he is worshiped and glorified. He has spoken through the Prophets. We believe in one holy catholic and apostolic Church. We acknowledge one baptism for the*

forgiveness of sins. We look for the resurrection of the dead, and the life of the world to come. (The Nicene Creed, 325 AD)

The Nicene Creed and every creed that followed, contradicts Paul's and the Apostle's teaching about the body of Christ and the present reality of God's dwelling spiritual place within humanity. Doctrines for example such as the virgin birth, the second coming, the bodily resurrection of the dead, the end of the world, the coming apocalypse, original sin, and so on, are so ingrained in the minds of most Christians, the creed is non-negotiable. It is interesting that while nearly all Protestant faiths once believed that the doctrines of Roman Catholicism were contrary to the Gospel of Christ, most Protestant faiths today accept the fundamental beliefs as set out within the creed.

While the secular and religious powers were working together in silencing the truth for fear of losing control of their numbers, here we see that true believers are 'caught up' within the spiritual presence of God and will forever remain with God 'in the air', not literally above in a future kingdom, but in the very presence of God and within the body of Christ in this present time (1 Thessalonians 4:17). Collectively, the dragon, the beast, the image of the beast, and the false prophet are the enemies of Christ that will continue to enforce moral laws, whether secular or religious. The false gospel ensures that when morality is finally at its breaking point, secular and moral laws are enforced rather than the teaching of Christ.

12:7   And there was war in heaven: Michael and his angels fought against the dragon; and the dragon fought and his angels,

12:8   And prevailed not; neither was their place found any more in heaven.

12:9   And the great dragon was cast out, that old serpent, called the Devil, and Satan, which deceiveth the whole world: he was cast out into the earth, and his angels were cast out with him.

If, as the scripture says, there is no name under heaven other than Christ Jesus, why then do many claim that Christ is called Michael? (Acts 4:12). It is more likely that Michael is a pseudonym for whoever is chosen from time to time to guard Israel from defeat, in this case, David the warrior king who won many physical battles over his enemies with military strength and physical swords. Jesus, by comparison, won his battles with the 'sword of the spirit'. David's sin of adultery and murder had led to his genuine repentance that guaranteed he would not be left in the grave but would be raised again through his own bloodline (Acts 2:22-37). The Psalms of David are a testimony to his sincere repentance and nature of his being. His sins were a sacrifice for all who sincerely repent, even of murder and adultery, but not without a price. Jesus whom was tempted in 'all points' as the rest of humanity, took the shame of what David had done to the cross. When Jesus had uttered David's psalm; *'My God, My God, why have you forsaken me'*, he was echoing his very own words a thousand years previously. (Psalm 22:1).

Both David's and Jesus' greatest battles were due to the rejection experienced at the hands of those within their own nation, evident by the anguish and despair in David's Psalms, and also in Jesus' anguish in the Garden of Gethsemane. Jesus may well have been physically and mentally defeated at the hands of his accusers during his grief in the Garden of Gethsemane, but in the end it was the knowledge he was doing the Father's will that gave him the strength and endurance to overcome his temptation to yield to the powers of darkness.

While Michael is also a pseudonym in the Old Testament book of Daniel, here we observe Jesus in the New testament as one who was born 'according to the flesh and through the seed of David', as both Michael and David in the person of Jesus, the Christ of God. Michael is also mentioned in the book of Jude as a leader who disputed with the powers of darkness over Moses' burial place. Had the whereabouts of Moses' grave been known, the Jews would certainly have preserved it as a shrine of remembrance to the laws of Moses. Here again we see the war between law and grace (Jude 1:9). Here we also observe the battle lines that are drawn between the flesh and the spirit.

> *For we wrestle not against flesh and blood, but against principalities, against powers, against the rulers of the darkness of this world, against spiritual wickedness in high places* (Ephesians 6:12)

The final victory was won by the figurative 'Michael and his angels' over the figurative 'Satan and his angels'. This language describes the conflict between law and grace, and shows how the powers of darkness are overcome by the knowledge of Christ.

12:10   And I heard a loud voice saying in heaven, Now is come salvation, and strength, and the kingdom of our God, and the power of his Christ: for the accuser of our brethren is cast down, which accused them before our God day and night.

12:11   And they overcame him by the blood of the Lamb, and by the word of their testimony; and they loved not their lives unto the death.

12:12   Therefore rejoice, ye heavens, and ye that dwell in them. Woe to the inhabiters of the earth and of the sea! for the devil is come down unto you, having great wrath, because he knoweth that he hath but a short time.

'Salvation, and strength, and the kingdom of our God, and the power of His Christ' was echoed on that historical day almost two thousand years ago when Jesus Christ won the victory over the powers of darkness. If Jesus Christ has liberated us from evil, why then are we still waiting to be set free? Can we not be alive to Christ now? God had spoken through the Son during those 'last days', and therefore there is nothing more to be fulfilled.

Note Paul's testimony regarding the finished work of Christ:

Who hath delivered us from the power of darkness, and hath translated us into the kingdom of his dear Son (Colossians 1:13).

And he is the head of the body, the church: who is the beginning, the firstborn from the dead; that in all things he might have the preeminence. For it pleased the Father that in him should all fullness dwell; And, having made peace through the blood of his cross, by him to reconcile all things unto himself; by him, I say, whether they be things in earth, or things in heaven. And you, that were sometime alienated and enemies in your mind by wicked works, yet now hath he reconciled In the body of his flesh through death, to present you holy and unblameable and unreproveable in his sight (Colossians 1:18-22).

Although many believers had their expectations realised before the end of the first century, Paul had to clear the confusion about the coming of Christ (2 Thessalonians 2:1, 2). His preaching often fell on deaf ears as many refused to see or even try to understand what 'the coming and appearance' of Christ meant:

But ye are come unto mount Sion, and unto the city of the living God, the heavenly Jerusalem, and to an innumerable company of angels, To the general assembly and church of the firstborn, which are written in heaven, and to God the Judge of all, and to the spirits of just men made perfect, And to Jesus the mediator of the new covenant, and to the blood of sprinkling, that speaketh better things than that of Abel (Hebrews 12:22-24).

The heavenly Jerusalem is here and now. Evil is created by the covetous and insecure souls who choose war, strife, murder and adultery instead of being guided by their Christ consciousness. The knowledge of Christ enables humanity to share in the goodness and nature of God through the power of the individual's own free will in resisting evil, symbolically called 'the Devil and Satan'.

'Salvation, power, and the kingdom and authority of Christ' was fulfilled when the veil between the holy and most holy place within the temple of Jerusalem was torn in two, signalling 'the end of all things'. Had the last Adam not been willing to win the victory over evil in the days of his flesh, the authority to rule would not have been handed to him. When Jesus said 'destroy this temple and in three days I will raise it up', the disciples at first did not understand. When they did finally understand which temple Jesus was speaking about, they had cause to rejoice. Soon after Pentecost they went forward with power and conviction in the face of torture and death.

12:13 And when the dragon saw that he was cast unto the earth, he persecuted the woman which brought forth the man child.

12:14 And to the woman were given two wings of a great eagle, that she might fly into the wilderness, into her place, where she is nourished for a time, and times, and half a time, from the face of the serpent.

As already noted, 'time, times, and half a time' relate to Daniel's prophecies about the oppression of God's people. It extends from his time until 'the time of the end' when the power of the holy people, the religion of Judaism, would be shattered (Daniel 7). The saints were called to be patient through a 'time of tribulation' until Christ was revealed (See comments on Mathew 24).

The building where God dwells is not an architectural work with impressive stained glass windows, steeples, religious idols and images, neither a building that needs to be attended by earthly priests with pomp and ceremony. The members of the true church are adorned inwardly with the spirit of Christ and with the robe of Christ's righteousness.

The church was in the wilderness in the true sense of the word, not in deserts and caves, but where they found peace, safety' and seclusion' fearing persecution. Similar to his 'wilderness church', Jesus often retired to a place of solitude where from under the stars he could feel the breeze, listen to the brook, and pray. The true church is now found wherever two or three are gathered in the Father's name (Matthew 18:20).

The woman who was 'given the wings of a great eagle that she might fly into the wilderness' refers to the 'one thousand, two hundred and sixty days'. This time period is mentioned only twice in the scriptures. In the previous chapter it was in relation to the 'two witnesses', while in this chapter it relates to Christ and the church of the firstborn.

12:15   And the serpent cast out of his mouth water as a flood after the woman, that he might cause her to be carried away of the flood.

12:16   And the earth helped the woman, and the earth opened her mouth, and swallowed up the flood which the dragon cast out of his mouth.

12:17   And the dragon was wroth with the woman, and went to make war with the remnant of her seed, which keep the commandments of God, and have the testimony of Jesus Christ.

Although the powers of darkness may try to overcome the world by intimidation and fear, it is from within the communities of the cities and villages throughout the nations of the world where those with common sense, regardless of beliefs, allow their inherent goodness to shine as lights in a dark place. Although evil seems to overtake the world as a 'flood', those who keep the testimony of Jesus Christ and have the spirit of the law written in their hearts, will overcome every obstacle that is put before them.

> *Then one of them, which was a lawyer, asked him a question, tempting him, and saying, Master, which is the great commandment in the law? Jesus said unto him, Thou shalt love the Lord thy God with all thy heart, and with all thy soul, and with all thy mind. This is the first and great commandment. And the second is like unto it, Thou shalt love thy neighbour as*

thyself. On these two commandments hang all the law and the prophets (Matthew 22:35-40).

Whatever evil we do, we will have the same measure of evil returned to us. But whatever measure of love we give, we will have the same measure of love returned (Luke 6:36-38).

REVELATION 13

13:1 And I stood upon the sand of the sea, and saw a beast rise up out of the sea, having seven heads and ten horns, and upon his horns ten crowns, and upon his heads the name of blasphemy.

Although the Jews and Romans were politically at odds, they were on guard whenever a new movement threatened their established practices. Both powers were on watch for anything that threatened to question and reform their beliefs, whether by peaceful or by violent means. The Pharisees took full advantage of Rome's fear of opposition and used it to ensure Jesus' crucifixion. Although Judea had been divided into ten provinces, the ten horns remain a symbol of the union between religion and state, then and now. In this vision, John describes the Judaic powers that answered to Rome. It is interesting to note that the ten crowns sitting on the ten horns share only seven heads. The seven heads highlight the opposing powers that ruled back then and continue to rule today with many dependant on secular governments for financial support.

Although this vision was fulfilled in the first century, the same principle is relevant today. Here we see 'the mystery of lawlessness' that was already at work in Jesus' time (2 Thessalonians 2:7). Just as the Jews answered to Herod, who in turn answered to Rome via the governor, there remains a similar hierarchy of discipline within religion and politics today. The early and mid-first century saw a time in which Judaism was keen to keep the peace with political

Rome to ensure its own safety. Herod was worried by the rumour of a newborn king and feared that the news may cause civil unrest. While this was a concern for religious and political leaders, the real tension surfaced when Jesus proclaimed that he would set free those in bondage to religion and law, but not once did Jesus incite a rebellion against Roman civil law.

Even though the early believers remained cautious of persecution, they nevertheless continued spreading the gospel from city to city. The 'dragon', a ferocious animal symbolised by the union of church and state, was intent on crushing Jesus' power and the influence he had on his followers. The dragon kept watch from every seaside port in the known world. Centres such as Ephesus, Corinth and Rome, had become favourite centres for the Apostle's preaching, especially Paul, who was committed to the Gospel of Christ. The book of Acts shows the extent of the threats and persecutions by both religious and secular authorities working hand in hand.

The dragon of Revelation 12:3 and the beast seen here are similar to Daniel's descriptions. While Daniel's vision relate only to the historical time, times, and dividing of time, and the identity of the beast, his vision culminates with just two events; the ultimate setting up of a spiritual kingdom of Christ and the church, and the setting up of a counterfeit church.

While outlining the successive kingdoms from the time of Babylon, the book of Daniel is primarily focused on the role of a messiah and the final destruction of Jerusalem. There is much speculation as to how the kingdoms of Babylon, Medo-Persia, Greece and Rome fit in with the images of John's vision, however, the focus of Daniel's visions are centred mainly on the events of the first century. While Daniel was shown in vision that one section of the four parts of the Roman power would occupy Judea, what he was shown next made him physically sick (Daniel 8:27). Daniel saw how his Jewish countrymen, assisted by a foreign empire, crucified the last of Israel's prophets.

Daniel's end time visions were being fulfilled when the Pharisees plotted against Jesus from the day he began his ministry with a healing on the Sabbath. Daniel saw that the nation of Israel was at this time annexed as part of the Roman Empire. This annexation resulted in the amalgamation of two powers; the dragon and beast that had set up the ten provinces within Judea, represented by seven political heads controlled from Rome. The vision of the beast with seven heads and ten horns and ten crowns is not restricted to the time of the early church. The 'beast' that is the union of religion and politics is typical of what will remain in power until the nations become one faith under the banner of Christ.

Paul and the Apostles knew that Judaism was allying with the political powers of the day, and aware that a counterfeit church would eventually be formed. The 'falling away' that Paul had predicted was in the making. Paul also knew it was essential for both church and state that 'peoples, *nations*, and tongues' would remain in bondage to law. This falling away from the truth saw the beginning of the Antichrist. Those with the knowledge of Christ kept themselves separate at all costs

> *Now we beseech you, brethren, by the coming of our Lord Jesus Christ, and by our gathering together unto him that ye be not soon shaken in mind, or be troubled, neither by spirit, nor by word, nor by letter as from us, as that the day of Christ is at hand. Let no man deceive you by any means: for that day shall not come, except there come a falling away first, and that man of sin be revealed, the son of perdition who opposeth and exalteth himself above all that is called God, or that is worshipped; so that he as God sitteth in the temple of God, shewing himself that he is God. Remember ye not, that, when I was yet with you, I told you these things and now ye know what withholdeth that he might be revealed in his time, for the mystery of iniquity doth already work: only he who now letteth will let, until he be taken out of the way (2 Thessalonians 2:1-7).*

13:2   And the beast which I saw was like unto a leopard, and his feet were as the feet of a bear, and his mouth as the mouth of a lion: and the dragon gave him his power, and his seat, and great authority.

> **13:3** And I saw one of his heads as it were wounded to death; and his deadly wound was healed: and all the world wondered after the beast.

Here we see the speed, strength, and power of those ready to crucify Jesus. The leopard represents the speed and urgency of those who plotted Jesus' death. The bear represents the power and strength of those who helped with the plot to crucify Jesus, and the lion represents the power that authorised the crucifixion.

Herod and his family, along with Caiaphas and those amongst the religion of Judaism, are symbols of the powers that are stumbling blocks to the truth of the gospels. The minds of those who oppose the truth of Christ and his church are the same. They are often wounded, but quickly healed. The issue here is not the identity of a single head being healed, but rather what may be observed in the union of religion and secular governments.

> **13:4** And they worshipped the dragon which gave power unto the beast: and they worshipped the beast, saying, Who is like unto the beast? who is able to make war with him?

Although the Scribes and Pharisees answered to the Sanhedrin in all matters judicial, the Roman governor sat on the judgment seat. Herod ensured that friendship with the Roman governor was paramount; therefore the majority of Jews praised their leaders for their friendship with the Herod family. This friendship ensured their safety in the event of an uprising by a minority of zealots plotting against the Roman occupation.

After Herod the Great died, the Jews remained friendly with Herod's son and remained free to worship and carry on with their normal religious activities and commerce. Jerusalem was a major centre of commerce and trading, therefore it was unthinkable to upset anyone who answered to Rome.

13:5 And there was given unto him a mouth speaking great things and blasphemies; and power was given unto him to continue forty and two months.

13:6 And he opened his mouth in blasphemy against God, to blaspheme his name, and his tabernacle, and them that dwell in heaven.

13:7 And it was given unto him to make war with the saints, and to overcome them: and power was given him over all kindreds, and tongues, and nations.

13:8 And all that dwell upon the earth shall worship him, whose names are not written in the book of life of the Lamb slain from the foundation of the world.

Dragons, beasts, and false prophets, are symbols of the ruling religious and political influences past, present, and future. Here we notice the identity of the powers that opposed the truth about Christ. Forty-two months was the enemy's allotted time that corresponded to Jesus' three-and-a-half year ministry, while the one thousand two hundred and sixty days marked the corresponding time for those who followed Christ. 'Time, times, and dividing of times' denotes the past, present, and future cycle of persecution that began with the infant church and will continue until people and nations become one faith.

Those who fulfil the law of Christ are here recorded in the Book of Life (Galatians 6:2). Our Christ consciousness is the book of life that holds everything unique about each of us.

13:9 If any man have an ear, let him hear.

13:10 He that leadeth into captivity shall go into captivity: he that killeth with the sword must be killed with the sword. Here is the patience and the faith of the saints.

Our attention is now drawn to those called to be patient. John the Baptist's beheading with the sword has a twofold meaning. He was the head of a body that was 'cut off' because of his powerful witnessing in the wilderness. When he uttered the words *'He must increase, but I must decrease'*, John acknowledged that there was one greater than he (John 3:30). History itself testifies to the ongoing 'killing with the sword' of those who would not conform to the doctrines of Antichrist. The physical slaying by the sword means certain death, whereas the spirit cannot be slain, even if the persecution is prolonged. From the first day Jesus began his ministry, the swords were out. No one knew how long it would be before the blood of the saints would be avenged or when Christ would be revealed; therefore patience was called for until all was fulfilled. It is worth noting Paul's remarks on this subject:

And not only so, but we glory in tribulations also: knowing that tribulation worketh patience; And patience, experience; and experience, hope: And hope maketh not ashamed; because the love of God is shed abroad in our hearts by the Holy Ghost which is given unto us (Romans 5:3-5).

13:11   And I beheld another beast coming up out of the earth; and he had two horns like a lamb, and he spake as a dragon.

13:12   And he exerciseth all the power of the first beast before him, and causeth the earth and them which dwell therein to worship the first beast, whose deadly wound was healed.

13:13   And he doeth great wonders, so that he maketh fire come down from heaven on the earth in the sight of men,

13:14   And deceiveth them that dwell on the earth by the means of those miracles which he had power to do in the sight of the beast; saying to them that dwell on the earth, that they should make an image to the beast, which had the wound by a sword, and did live.

13:15 And he had power to give life unto the image of the beast, that the image of the beast should both speak, and cause that as many as would not worship the image of the beast should be killed.

13:16 And he causeth all, both small and great, rich and poor, free and bond, to receive a mark in their right hand, or in their foreheads:

13:17 And that no man might buy or sell, save he that had the mark, or the name of the beast, or the number of his name.

13:18 Here is wisdom. Let him that hath understanding count the number of the beast: for it is the number of a man; and his number is Six hundred threescore and six.

Caligula and Mark Antony helped to set up Herod Antipas to rule over the Jews. No doubt Herod's son exercised the same authority given to his father. Fire from heaven is usually synonymous with the 'spirit and power' witnessed with the preaching of Elijah and John the Baptist, yet here it represents the persecution and tribulation that the beast from 'out of the earth' caused under the direction and influence of the Pharisees and those who aligned themselves with the Herod family.

To this day we witness images of dictators that are adored, yet this form of adoration is usually motivated by fear and intimidation. The Herod's had become objects of worship out of fear only because anyone who failed to honour the Herod family, whether Jew or Gentile, would have had difficulty buying and selling and going about their daily commerce and business. The same principle applies today in countries where religious and secular powers unite to keep citizens subjugated by fear.

Jerusalem had become a city of enormous wealth and commerce, owing much to the convenience of a seaside port with an easily accessible trade route to its gates. Around the time Jesus was born, the Caesars had introduced taxes much to the advantage of the Herod family. The beast, the 'image of the beast', the dragon and 'false prophet' are symbols of the collective powers that will continue to oppose the truth. To be wounded by the sword is to be wounded by 'the Spirit and Word of God':

> *For the word of God is quick, and powerful, and sharper than any twoedged sword, piercing even to the dividing asunder of soul and spirit, and of the joints and marrow, and is a discerner of the thoughts and intents of the heart* (Hebrews 4:12).

The friendship between religious leaders such as Caiaphas and the Herod family is commonplace to this day. Officials within all walks of religion still influence government policies. They remain in power because politicians know votes can be swayed by religious leaders that have an influence over their congregations. However, the main problem is that while many depend on government support, they are also in bondage to the rules and regulations of the governing bodies that support them. Most of the world's inhabitants are controlled by governments, financial institutions, or held captive by religion. Bondage and slavery appear in many guises.

This calls for understanding because 'the church of the firstborn' was known for its patience and faith. On one side are those who pursue the glitz and glamour of this world, content in their indebtedness to 'beastly powers', while others, not necessarily believers, are wise enough to know that greed and ambition is an endless road. This chapter holds a promise for those who love righteousness, while those who pursue evil rather than good will symbolically fade away.

We should be careful not to interpret numerical values of individual names that correspond with the number 666. The Greek word for 'man' ἀνθρώπου (anthropou), is not necessarily a single person. It is often used as an abstract word for man, as in 'humanity'. Through each century there has been much debate as to who or what best fits the number of the beast. 666 represent three individual numbers of six. The dragon, the beast, and the false prophet, all bear the mark that falls short of 7. Number 6 is first mentioned in Genesis as the

6th day of creation as an incomplete number. Although the physical works of creation were completed by the end of the 6th day, it was on the 7th day that God had rested from all his works of creation. The 7th day had no need for an 'evening and morning' that marked a limited time; hence the number 6 falls short of completeness.

> *Let us therefore fear, lest, a promise being left us of entering into his rest, any of you should seem to come short of it. For unto us was the Gospel preached, as well as unto them: but the word preached did not profit them, not being mixed with faith in them that heard it. For we which have believed do enter into rest, as he said, As I have sworn in my wrath, if they shall enter into my rest: although the works were finished from the foundation of the world. For he spake in a certain place of the seventh day on this wise, And God did rest the seventh day from all his works. And in this place again, If they shall enter into my rest. Seeing therefore it remaineth that some must enter therein, and they to whom it was first preached entered not in because of unbelief: Again, he limiteth a certain day, saying in David, To day, after so long a time; as it is said, To day if ye will hear his voice, harden not your hearts. For if Jesus had given them rest, then would he not afterward have spoken of another day. There remaineth therefore a rest to the people of God* (Hebrews 4:1-9).

REVELATION 14

14:1 And I looked, and, lo, a Lamb stood on the mount Sion, and with him an hundred forty and four thousand, having his Father's name written in their foreheads.

14:2 And I heard a voice from heaven, as the voice of many waters, and as the voice of a great thunder: and I heard the voice of harpers harping with their harps:

14:3 And they sung as it were a new song before the throne, and before the four beasts, and the elders: and no man could learn that song but the hundred and forty and four thousand, which were redeemed from the earth.

14:4 These are they which were not defiled with women; for they are virgins. These are they which follow the Lamb whithersoever he goeth. These were redeemed from among men, being the firstfruits unto God and to the Lamb.

14:5 And in their mouth was found no guile: for they are without fault before the throne of God.

The 144,000 are the 'first fruits' from amongst Israel who have been redeemed and are now 'alive to Christ'. The name of the Father is written on each forehead because they acknowledge one God. Although Paul's letters speak of Israel as a nation that rejected the Son, here we see that God has a remnant amongst Israel as described by Paul in his letter to the church at Rome:

> *Even so then, at this present time there is a remnant according to the election of grace* (Romans 11:5).

These are the redeemed among Israel who have accepted the Christ of God; therefore they recognise the Son and the Father as one. There are only two classes of people; those who have the 'mark of the beast' written on their foreheads, and those with the Father's name written on their foreheads.

In this chapter we read of a 'new song', while the following chapter shows how those with the faith of Jesus are heard singing 'the Song of Moses' and 'the Song of the Lamb'. The remnant of Israel is heard singing here because they are rejoicing knowing that Jesus is the Lamb of God who has opened the door to the gospel of grace. They are singing the song of the Lamb because they realise that the finished work of Jesus Christ has given them the confidence to walk in the spirit and within the presence of a holy God. More important, they are symbolised as 'virgins' because they are clothed with the garment of 'the righteousness of Christ'.

14:6 And I saw another angel fly in the midst of heaven, having the everlasting Gospel to preach unto them that dwell on the earth, and to every nation, and kindred, and tongue, and people,

14:7 Saying with a loud voice, Fear God, and give glory to him; for the hour of his judgment is come: and worship him that made heaven, and earth, and the sea, and the fountains of waters.

14:8 And there followed another angel, saying, Babylon is fallen, is fallen, that great city, because she made all nations drink of the wine of the wrath of her fornication.

14:9 And the third angel followed them, saying with a loud voice, If any man worship the beast and his image, and receive his mark in his forehead, or in his hand,

---

14:10 The same shall drink of the wine of the wrath of God, which is poured out without mixture into the cup of his indignation; and he shall be tormented with fire and brimstone in the presence of the holy angels, and in the presence of the Lamb:

The first angel proclaims the 'everlasting gospel' to every nation kindred and tongue. Our attention is then drawn to *'Him who made the heavens, the earth, and sea, and springs of water'*. The angel here reminds us that without the creative works of God there would be no natural world to enjoy. Paul's letter to the Romans speaks about those not giving praise to 'the invisible God' for bringing forth 'the visible things' of this world (Romans 1: 19-21).

The second angel warns of the impending judgment on Jerusalem, symbolically named Babylon. The fate of the city was sealed when the Jews crucified Jesus, the last and final prophet. The 'fornications' were exposed long before Jesus had begun teaching in the regions of Judea. Isaiah, Ezekiel, Jeremiah and many other minor prophets before Jesus had warned Jerusalem of her impending doom because of her 'adulterous ways':

> *For of old time I have broken thy yoke, and burst thy bands; and thou saidst, I will not transgress; when upon every high hill and under every green tree thou wanderest, playing the harlot* (Jeremiah 2:20).

> *But thou didst trust in thine own beauty, and playedst the harlot because of thy renown, and pouredst out thy fornications on every one that passed by; his it was* (Ezekiel 16:15).

> *How is the faithful city become an harlot! it was full of judgment; righteousness lodged in it; but now murderers. Thy silver is become dross, thy wine mixed with water: Thy princes are rebellious, and companions of thieves: every one loveth gifts, and followeth after rewards: they judge not the fatherless, neither doth the cause of the widow come unto them* (Isaiah 1:21-23).

Because of the multitude of the whoredoms of the wellfavoured harlot, the mistress of witchcrafts, that selleth nations through her whoredoms, and families through her witchcrafts. Behold, I am against thee, saith the Lord of hosts; and I will discover thy skirts upon thy face, and I will shew the nations thy nakedness, and the kingdoms thy shame (Nahum 3:4-5).

The third angel carries a message specifically aimed at the core of the gospel message. In this vision 'the beast and its image' attempted to establish religion with it ceremony and rituals as a means of righteousness. The line had to be drawn between choosing 'the traditions of men' or 'the faith of Jesus'. This message was for those who compromised their faith and rejected the invitation to get ready to flee Jerusalem.

14:11 And the smoke of their torment ascendeth up for ever and ever: and they have no rest day nor night, who worship the beast and his image, and whosoever receiveth the mark of his name.

14:12 Here is the patience of the saints: here are they that keep the commandments of God, and the faith of Jesus.

14:13 And I heard a voice from heaven saying unto me, Write, Blessed are the dead which die in the Lord from henceforth: Yea, saith the Spirit, that they may rest from their labours; and their works do follow them.

'The smoke of their torment' is the only evidence left of what had been destroyed. Unfortunately Israel did not heed the lesson. Those who have 'no rest day or night' are those who ignore what the trials of life are trying to teach them. We are free to reject Christ and worship the symbolic 'beast and its image', or we are free to follow our God-given Christ consciousness as a guide.

The 'works that follow' are the works of 'faith and love' that form the character. From generation to generation we are born again, either 'inside' or 'outside' the Kingdom of God. The spirit returns in a new body that either grows from strength to strength or weakens by ignoring the lessons put before us.

Those who endured the great tribulation between the time of Jesus' ministry and the time of the consummation that marked 'the end of the world' and 'the end of all things', are here given an assurance that 'their works would follow'.

14:14 And I looked, and behold a white cloud, and upon the cloud one sat like unto the Son of man, having on his head a golden crown, and in his hand a sharp sickle.

14:15 And another angel came out of the temple, crying with a loud voice to him that sat on the cloud, Thrust in thy sickle, and reap: for the time is come for thee to reap; for the harvest of the earth is ripe.

14:16 And he that sat on the cloud thrust in his sickle on the earth; and the earth was reaped.

14:17 And another angel came out of the temple which is in heaven, he also having a sharp sickle.

14:18 And another angel came out from the altar, which had power over fire; and cried with a loud cry to him that had the sharp sickle, saying, Thrust in thy sharp sickle, and gather the clusters of the vine of the earth; for her grapes are fully ripe.

14:19 And the angel thrust in his sickle into the earth, and gathered the vine of the earth, and cast it into the great winepress of the wrath of God.

This scene takes us back to the discourse on the Mount of Olives, the time when 'the end of the age' was being signalled. When Jerusalem was finally destroyed, Israel's judgment was fulfilled. Since Pentecost, almost forty years had passed while the followers of Jesus sowed the gospel seed throughout Judea and the known world. It was now harvest time where the wheat and the tares would be separated (Matthew 13:24-30).

The call to 'come out of Babylon' was a call to flee Jerusalem because it had figuratively become like Sodom and Egypt (Revelation 11:8). The 'latter rains' had begun to fall, ensuring that harvest time would be plentiful (Joel 2:23). The clusters were in the winepress and ready to be trampled which typified the persecution the believers would be subject to before the new wine was produced.

The Old Testament book of Joel possibly reveals more about the timing of the end of the age than any other Old Testament book. The end of the first century was a pivotal point that saw the transformation of the old physical Jerusalem to the spiritually New Jerusalem. Joel had warned Israel that although there would be a complete destruction of Jerusalem, there was also to be a time of restitution and a time of refreshing. At Pentecost, the Apostle Peter reminded the congregation of all that was happening in their day that was prophesied by Joel (Acts 2:14-21). Joel's predictions are central to Israel's understanding of the messages of the book of Revelations. The book of Joel begins with the warning of an impending judgment in the wake of the gospel dispensation. Joel describes in graphic detail Jerusalem's fate since rejecting its last prophet while also describing what happens in the aftermath of their denial of Jesus Christ's message (Joel 2:1-32).

It is a mistake to apply Joel's prophecy to our day. What happened at Pentecost and Jerusalem signalled the end of the age that saw the beginning of the gospel dispensation. Joel's prophecy of Israel's impending doom holds an invaluable insight into the events from the time of Jesus' crucifixion to the destruction of Jerusalem in 70 A.D followed by the outpouring of the Holy Spirit at Pentecost. Notice the language of Joel concerning the impending judgment that was to fall on Jerusalem.

> *Blow ye the trumpet in Zion, and sound an alarm in my holy mountain: let all the inhabitants of the land tremble: for the day of the LORD cometh, for it is nigh at hand; A day of darkness*

and of gloominess, a day of clouds and of thick darkness, as the morning spread upon the mountains: a great people and a strong; there hath not been ever the like, neither shall be any more after it, even to the years of many generations (Joel 2:1-2)

The earth shall quake before them; the heavens shall tremble: the sun and the moon shall be dark, and the stars shall withdraw their shining (Joel 2:10)

And it shall come to pass afterward, that I will pour out my spirit upon all flesh; and your sons and your daughters shall prophesy, your old men shall dream dreams, your young men shall see visions: And also upon the servants and upon the handmaids in those days will I pour out my spirit. And I will shew wonders in the heavens and in the earth, blood, and fire, and pillars of smoke. The sun shall be turned into darkness, and the moon into blood, before the great and terrible day of the Lord come. And it shall come to pass, that whosoever shall call on the name of the Lord shall be delivered: for in mount Zion and in Jerusalem shall be deliverance, as the Lord hath said, and in the remnant whom the Lord shall call (Joel 28-32)

14:20 And the winepress was trodden without the city, and blood came out of the winepress, even unto the horse bridles, by the space of a thousand and six hundred furlongs.

The changing of water into wine at the wedding feast was a 'sign' that marked the beginning of all things that were to become new. The wedding feast that Jesus had attended was the prelude to a greater celebration that was to be the marriage of Christ and the church. The blood spilt by Jesus outside the city, plus the blood spilt by all the previous prophets within the regions of Judea, measured a distance of 1,600 furlongs, or forty square miles, denoting the geographical area within and outside Jerusalem. The mention of blood 'even unto the horse's bridles' refers to the extent of the persecution against Jesus and the prophets. Figuratively speaking, it was the blood of the saints that had hindered the horses while carrying those who took the gospel to the known world. However, the spilling of blood did not end in Judea. From the second century until the end of the reformation, history attests to the way the beastly powers continued torturing and killing hundreds and thousands, perhaps millions, of those with the courage to reject the teaching of Antichrist.

REVELATION 15

15:1 And I saw another sign in heaven, great and marvellous, seven angels having the seven last plagues; for in them is filled up the wrath of God.

15:2 And I saw as it were a sea of glass mingled with fire: and them that had gotten the victory over the beast, and over his image, and over his mark, and over the number of his name, stand on the sea of glass, having the harps of God.

15:3 And they sing the song of Moses the servant of God, and the song of the Lamb, saying, Great and marvellous are thy works, Lord God Almighty; just and true are thy ways, thou King of saints.

15:4 Who shall not fear thee, O Lord, and glorify thy name? for thou only art holy: for all nations shall come and worship before thee; for thy judgments are made manifest.

Although on the surface John's visions appear as something fearful, the reader is reminded that the visions are a 'blessing to all who read and understand' (Revelation 1:3). Having observed 'the sea of glass' in Revelation 4:6, John is now shown 'the sea mingled with fire'. The fire here denotes the trials and tribulations the believers went through before their final victory over the forces of darkness. The sea of glass, although mingled with fire, denotes a picture of calmness from where the believers are now singing the Song of Moses. They are rejoicing because they are no longer under a pillar of fire. They are also singing the Song of the Lamb, a new song that expresses their joy of being subject to Christ rather than law. Again we are reminded that God's day of wrath and judgment against Israel has been accomplished.

15:5 And after that I looked, and, behold, the temple of the tabernacle of the testimony in heaven was opened:

The tabernacle that Moses built in the wilderness was only 'a copy of the true tabernacle'. Had the Israelites been a nation of faith that believed as Abraham had, there would not have been any need for a temporary tent that represented the presence of God. Although the earthly sanctuary replicated the work of reconciliation, it was never meant to be a permanent structure. The earthly tabernacle with its rituals and ceremony could only point forward to a time when Christ Jesus was to offer his own blood and become high priest of a better covenant.

> *For every high priest is ordained to offer gifts and sacrifices: wherefore it is of necessity that this man have somewhat also to offer. For if he were on earth, he should not be a priest, seeing that there are priests that offer gifts according to the law: Who serve unto the example and shadow of heavenly things, as Moses was admonished of God when he was about to make the tabernacle: for, See, saith he, that thou make all things according to the pattern shewed to thee in the mount.*
>
> *But now hath he obtained a more excellent ministry, by how much also he is the mediator of a better covenant, which was established upon better promises. For if that first covenant had been faultless, then should no place have been sought for the second.*
>
> *For finding fault with them, he saith, Behold, the days come, saith the Lord, when I will make a new covenant with the house of Israel and with the house of Judah: Not according to the covenant that I made with their fathers in the day when I took them by the hand to lead them out of the land of Egypt; because they continued not in my covenant, and I regarded*

them not, saith the Lord. For this is the covenant that I will make with the house of Israel after those days, saith the Lord; I will put my laws into their mind, and write them in their hearts: and I will be to them a God, and they shall be to me a people: And they shall not teach every man his neighbour, and every man his brother, saying, Know the Lord: for all shall know me, from the least to the greatest. For I will be merciful to their unrighteousness, and their sins and their iniquities will I remember no more. In that he saith, A new covenant, he hath made the first old. Now that which decayeth and waxeth old is ready to vanish away (Hebrews 8:3-13).

The most holy place that was once only accessible to an earthly high priest is now open to all. God's holy place is within the heart of those who love as Jesus Christ loved. All with the faith of Jesus are priests of God (Revelation 1:6, 5:10).

Know ye not that ye are the temple of God, and that the Spirit of God dwelleth in you? (1 Corinthians 3:16).

15:6 And the seven angels came out of the temple, having the seven plagues, clothed in pure and white linen, and having their breasts girded with golden girdles.

15:7 And one of the four beasts gave unto the seven angels seven golden vials full of the wrath of God, who liveth for ever and ever.

15:8 And the temple was filled with smoke from the glory of God, and from his power; and no man was able to enter into the temple, till the seven plagues of the seven angels were fulfilled.

The Apostles of the seven churches are seen here clothed in more glorious apparel than were the priests of the Old Testament. The golden bowls that represent the vessels containing the 'wrath of God' are the trials and tribulations turned into blessings by those with the faith of Jesus. Timothy, Titus, Philemon, James, Peter, John and Jude are testimonies of seven men who went through the trials of life yet did not lose heart through the obstacles that beset them.

The establishment of the church of the firstborn was not without setbacks. The persecutions and threats of death were the refining processes that had given the church its solid foundation. God's dwelling place would not have been open to us if it were not for the victory of the early church and the work of those who endured what the plagues symbolise. Jesus had warned believers that the love of many would wax cold and many would betray one another. The plagues are a reminder that while the spirit refines and works on the heart and mind, the believer can endure whatever physical trials are set before them.:

> *Beloved, think it not strange concerning the fiery trial which is to try you, as though some strange thing happened unto you: But rejoice, inasmuch as ye are partakers of Christ's sufferings; that, when his glory shall be revealed, ye may be glad also with exceeding joy* (1 Peter 4:12-13).

REVELATION 16

16:1 And I heard a great voice out of the temple saying to the seven angels, Go your ways, and pour out the vials of the wrath of God upon the earth.

16:2 And the first went, and poured out his vial upon the earth; and there fell a noisome and grievous sore upon the men which had the mark of the beast, and upon them which worshipped his image.

The 'noisome and grievous sore' is figurative of all who pursue evil rather than good. The actions and words we speak reveal what is in the heart and mind. The Old Testament story of Job's festering sores from his head to the soles of his feet are a reminder that even in the face of plagues our faith may overcome the world:

For whatsoever is born of God overcometh the world: and this is the victory that overcometh the world, even our faith (1 John 5:4).

The spiritual battles between the flesh and the spirit begin in the mind that is seated behind the forehead. Humanity has much to learn about the power of the mind regarding the afflictions of the flesh. If the mind is tormented by the fears and cares of this world, the flesh often protests with all manner of physical ailments.

The earth represents all that is physical, while 'heaven' represents all that is spiritual. The plagues poured from the vials are poured on those on the earth who would rather cling to all that is earthly and temporary rather than all that is spiritual and permanent. Many like Job have been afflicted, yet blessed by the experience of their affliction.

16:3 And the second angel poured out his vial upon the sea; and it became as the blood of a dead man: and every living soul died in the sea.

16:4 And the third angel poured out his vial upon the rivers and fountains of waters; and they became blood.

16:5 And I heard the angel of the waters say, Thou art righteous, O Lord, which art, and wast, and shalt be, because thou hast judged thus.

16:6 For they have shed the blood of saints and prophets, and thou hast given them blood to drink; for they are worthy.

16:7 And I heard another out of the altar say, Even so, Lord God Almighty, true and righteous are thy judgments.

Notice that the sea, rivers, and fountains, did not actually turn into blood but rather *'became as the blood of a dead man'*. If the body is dead, the blood becomes useless. Most living things, whether on the earth, in the sea, river, or springs, regenerate life through the blood. The life in the blood is here brought to our attention because we have been redeemed through and by the blood that brought the promised seed into the world. This chapter reveals how Israel's shedding of the blood of the saints and prophets was about to be avenged.

16:8 And the fourth angel poured out his vial upon the sun; and power was given unto him to scorch men with fire.

16:9 And men were scorched with great heat, and blasphemed the name of God, which hath power over these plagues: and they repented not to give him glory.

Jesus' chastising of the Scribes and Pharisees was due to their lack of compassion and mercy towards the poor. The truths of Jesus' words were a torment to those religious rulers who neglected those less fortunate. The Scribes and Pharisees feared losing control of those who 'received the word gladly' and were ready to follow what was at the very heart of Jesus' parables. His rebukes regarding their lack of compassion for the poor and broken-hearted was one thing, but claiming authority to forgive sins brought things to a head. The Pharisees' resentment, like that of Cain, turned to rage, and then to murder. Although they charged Jesus with blasphemy, the Scribes and Pharisees themselves were blaspheming by accusing Jesus of doing works through the power of Beelzebub. The words of Jesus are here symbolised as words with the power to scorch with heat just as the rays of the sun can scorch the earth with heat. Israel's redeemer was rejected simply because of what he was proclaiming about the Kingdom of God.

16:10 And the fifth angel poured out his vial upon the seat of the beast; and his kingdom was full of darkness; and they gnawed their tongues for pain,

16:11 And blasphemed the God of heaven because of their pains and their sores, and repented not of their deeds.

Jerusalem was the central place of worship where those oppressed by the burden of law were set free by Jesus. While the religious leaders continued to blaspheme the Son of God, they knew Jesus was no ordinary man, since his teachings caused them so much anguish and pain. They 'gnawed their tongues' because they knew the truth of his words, especially when Jesus described them as whitewashed tombs clean on the outside but filthy on the inside (Matthew 23:27, 28).

16:12 And the sixth angel poured out his vial upon the great river Euphrates; and the water thereof was dried up, that the way of the kings of the east might be prepared.

16:13 And I saw three unclean spirits like frogs come out of the mouth of the dragon, and out of the mouth of the beast, and out of the mouth of the false prophet.

16:14 For they are the spirits of devils, working miracles, which go forth unto the kings of the earth and of the whole world, to gather them to the battle of that great day of God Almighty.

16:15 Behold, I come as a thief. Blessed is he that watcheth, and keepeth his garments, lest he walk naked, and they see his shame.

16:16 And he gathered them together into a place called in the Hebrew tongue Armageddon.

The Kings of the East here symbolise the Apostles and those with the 'faith of Jesus' who began to take the Gospel of Christ to the known world. Jesus had warned the inhabitants of Judea that when they saw Jerusalem surrounded by armies they were to flee for their lives. The 'drying up of the Euphrates signified that a way was made for the Roman army to cross the river, while the water that was once as abundant as Jesus' words, had vaporized and turned into ice that had symbolized many of the Jews coldness towards Jesus.

The religious 'beast' that had stoned and killed the prophets who spoke against her hypocrisies was now under the authority of the dragon. The three 'unclean spirits like frogs' that came out of 'the mouth of the dragon, beast, and false prophet, are not three separate spirits, but one unclean spirit that preaches the false gospel of Christ to this very day.

Almost two thousand years ago at Armageddon, the Roman general Titus gathered his legions to prepare for the destruction of Jerusalem. It should be emphasised here that John did not actually see a battle at Armageddon, but rather 'a gathering together' of an army, outside Jerusalem preparing to besiege and destroy the city.

During the time of the Apostles, many people were betraying one another while the love of many others grew cold. When those who had prepared for this day heard rumours of the Roman army gathering outside Jerusalem, they knew that the Day of Judgment was imminent. The warning to flee the city was scoffed at by those who mocked the believers, while those with the faith of Jesus and symbolically clothed with the garments of righteousness, knew that they would not be caught ashamed or naked. The lesson here is that plagues, whether past, present or future, have no power over those who pursue good rather than evil.

16:17 And the seventh angel poured out his vial into the air; and there came a great voice out of the temple of heaven, from the throne, saying, It is done.

16:18 And there were voices, and thunders, and lightnings; and there was a great earthquake, such as was not since men were upon the earth, so mighty an earthquake, and so great.

16:19 And the great city was divided into three parts, and the cities of the nations fell: and great Babylon came in remembrance before God, to give unto her the cup of the wine of the fierceness of his wrath.

16:20 And every island fled away, and the mountains were not found.

16:21 And there fell upon men a great hail out of heaven, every stone about the weight of a talent: and men blasphemed God because of the plague of the hail; for the plague thereof was exceeding great.

The great tribulation culminated with the destruction of Jerusalem at which time Christ was revealed within the hearts and minds of believers. It had been forty years since Jesus uttered those final words 'It is finished'. Now it was time for one of the seven angels to shout through the air, 'It is done', signifying the time that all things that had been prophesied had come to an end.

The Day of Judgment had arrived when Jerusalem, by now a symbol of the old Babylon, was remembered before God. The great city that was divided into three parts represented the remaining powers with their roots in the law rather than in Christ. Although the term Judaic Christianity is a relatively recent term, Catholicism with its roots in pagan Rome, and Judaism with its roots in law, are the powers that gave rise to Judaic Christianity.

The disappearance of the islands and mountains represents how the knowledge of Christ removes all obstacles and opposition to the truth. As noted, the evaporation of the Euphrates river made way for the Roman army. What was once resourceful was transformed into vapour and ice as a symbol of the coldness of Israel. Although the plagues are figurative, if one follows a good conscience, the plagues are ineffective and powerless.

REVELATION 17

17:1 And there came one of the seven angels which had the seven vials, and talked with me, saying unto me, Come hither; I will shew unto thee the judgment of the great whore that sitteth upon many waters:

17:2 With whom the kings of the earth have committed fornication, and the inhabitants of the earth have been made drunk with the wine of her fornication.

17:3 So he carried me away in the spirit into the wilderness: and I saw a woman sit upon a scarlet coloured beast, full of names of blasphemy, having seven heads and ten horns.

17:4 And the woman was arrayed in purple and scarlet colour, and decked with gold and precious stones and pearls, having a golden cup in her hand full of abominations and filthiness of her fornication:

17:5 And upon her forehead was a name written, Mystery, Babylon The Great, The Mother Of Harlots And Abominations Of The Earth.

The judgment of Israel, here symbolized by 'The Mother Of Harlots' was predicted centuries previously by the Old Testament prophet Daniel. Notice the following:

> *Seventy weeks are determined upon thy people and upon thy holy city, to finish the transgression, and to make an end of sins, and to make reconciliation for iniquity, and to bring in everlasting righteousness, and to seal up the vision and prophecy, and to anoint the most Holy (Daniel 9:24).*

'Everlasting righteousness' is directly related to the righteousness of Christ. Neither Jew nor Gentile can be saved by keeping the law; hence 'the righteousness of Christ' is imputed to all who follow their God given Christ consciousness.

> *But now the righteousness of God without the law is manifested, being witnessed by the law and the prophets; Even the righteousness of God which is by faith of Jesus Christ unto all and upon all them that believe: for there is no difference: For all have sinned, and come short of the glory of God; (Romans 3:21,22).*

Jesus had sealed Daniel's vision when he had uttered the words *'It is finished'* (John 19:30). Everything Daniel had prophesied had culminated when Jesus had 'finished the transgression and put an end to sin'. In this chapter John is shown the destiny of those who are intent on putting law above Christ. While in chapter twelve the 'dragon' that was about to devour the infant church has seven heads, ten horns, and seven crowns upon his heads depicting the union of secular and religious powers, here we notice a different woman sitting on 'a scarlet coloured beast' with 'seven heads and ten horns' but no mention of 'crowns'. Horns are used as symbols of strength and supremacy for both good and evil while crowns are symbolized as secular powers that carry Judaism. Both the beast and the woman are scarlet coloured because of the blood they had spilt.

Jerusalem had become a symbol of Babylon because of the wealth it had generated within the commerce generated within the walls of Jerusalem's temple. It had become an abomination to God, not only because of the religious leader's neglect of the poor, but how Mosaic Law was used to intimidate and rule by fear and bondage. The rule of law will always remain ineffectual in changing behaviour.

The golden cup of abominations shows just how deep law remains an integral part of religion as a means of righteousness.

17:6 And I saw the woman drunken with the blood of the saints, and with the blood of the martyrs of Jesus: and when I saw her, I wondered with great admiration.

17:7 And the angel said unto me, Wherefore didst thou marvel? I will tell thee the mystery of the woman, and of the beast that carrieth her, which hath the seven heads and ten horns.

17:8 The beast that thou sawest was, and is not; and shall ascend out of the bottomless pit, and go into perdition: and they that dwell on the earth shall wonder, whose names were not written in the book of life from the foundation of the world, when they behold the beast that was, and is not, and yet is.

Although 'the universal apostolic church' appears to represent Christ by its words, by its deeds it does the opposite. This chapter reveals the roots and the identity of the Antichrist that goes hand in hand with chapter twelve, where the union between Judaism, secular powers, and those who had 'fallen away' had merged.

> *Let no man deceive you by any means: for that day shall not come, except there come a falling away first, and that man of sin be revealed, the son of perdition* (2 Thessalonians 2:3).

There would not have been an institutionalized Christian church at the beginning of the fourth century without the power of political Rome. Here we see the union of Judaism and those who had fallen away with the Roman Empire under a different guise. Judaism with its roots in law had over time influenced many Christians to uphold the Ten Commandments as a guide to righteousness which in time had formed what is known today as Judaic Christianity.

Again, like chapter twelve, we are reminded of 'beasts' that come and go, yet reappear from time to time throughout history. Symbolically, both Babylon and Rome have re-emerged as powers in a different guise that oppose everything Christ stands for. They are the powers of Antichrist that *'was, and is not, and shall ascend out of the bottomless pit'*.

17:9 And here is the mind which hath wisdom. The seven heads are seven mountains, on which the woman sitteth.

Mountains throughout the Old Testament are places where Israel met with God. Ezekiel speaks of the mountains of Israel:

> *And the word of the Lord came unto me, saying, Son of man, set thy face toward the mountains of Israel, and prophesy against them, And say, Ye mountains of Israel, hear the word of the Lord God; Thus saith the Lord God to the mountains, and to the hills, to the rivers, and to the valleys; Behold, I, even I, will bring a sword upon you, and I will destroy your high places. And your altars shall be desolate, and your images shall be broken: and I will cast down your slain men before your idols. And I will lay the dead carcases of the children of Israel before their idols; and I will scatter your bones round about your altars. In all your dwellingplaces the cities shall be laid waste, and the high places shall be desolate; that your altars may be laid waste and made desolate, and your idols may be broken and cease, and your images may be cut down, and your works may be abolished. And the slain shall fall in the midst of you, and ye shall know that I am the Lord. Yet will I leave a remnant, that ye may have some that shall escape the sword among the nations, when ye shall be scattered through the countries. And they that escape of you shall remember me among the nations whither they shall be carried captives, because I am broken with their whorish heart, which hath departed from me, and with their eyes, which go a whoring after their idols: and they shall lothe themselves for the evils which they have committed in all their abominations. And they shall know that I am the Lord, and that I have not said in vain that I would do this evil unto them. Thus saith the Lord God; Smite with thine hand, and stamp with thy foot, and say,*

Alas for all the evil abominations of the house of Israel! for they shall fall by the sword, by the famine, and by the pestilence. He that is far off shall die of the pestilence; and he that is near shall fall by the sword; and he that remaineth and is besieged shall die by the famine: thus will I accomplish my fury upon them. Then shall ye know that I am the Lord, when their slain men shall be among their idols round about their altars, upon every high hill, in all the tops of the mountains, and under every green tree, and under every thick oak, the place where they did offer sweet savour to all their idols. So will I stretch out my hand upon them, and make the land desolate, yea, more desolate than the wilderness toward Diblath, in all their habitations: and they shall know that I am the Lord (Ezekiel 6: 1-14).

The seven mountains are symbolic of the geographical locations of ancient Israel that marks the area in which the gospel was first preached. The mountains are the seat of power from where the beast and the 'image of the beast' had merged. The beast that carried the woman was seated at Jerusalem, while the 'image of the beast' was seated in Rome. It was between and around the regions of Jerusalem and Rome that first-century Christians faced torture and death.

'The 'mind which has wisdom' is to draw the believer's attention to the origin and identity of the beast and its image and to ensure that what was revealed was to be guarded closely for the preservation of the truth.

17:10 And there are seven kings: five are fallen, and one is, and the other is not yet come; and when he cometh, he must continue a short space.

17:11 And the beast that was, and is not, even he is the eighth, and is of the seven, and goeth into perdition.

The seven kings are directly connected with the seven heads and seven mountains. Six earthly kingdoms such as Assyria, Egypt, Babylon, Medo-Persia, Greece, Rome, had shaped and influenced the destiny of religion and politics, but eventually collapsed. The seventh kingdom was Rome disguised as Christianity. The eighth kingdom that had gone into perdition would re-emerge as Judaic Christianity. The eighth kingdom remains the empire of Rome, only in a different form. Of all the powers that have come and gone, nothing has equalled the power of what we have today with Rome's authority and power over Judaic Christianity.

Whatever differences the Catholics and Protestants have today, ultimately both will agree that 'the rule of law', whether civil or religious will be the only means of controlling the masses. The Roman power had deliberately set aside the truth about Christ, and will oppose any religion that defies the wording of the creed. Although Judaic Christianity has crucified Christ for the second time, one thing will always remain; Christ within is the hope of glory; therefore the Kingdom of God of which Jesus had described as something that is 'within' cannot be broken.

Christianity today is led by a Roman pope accepted by many as God's representative on earth. From this seat of power, most of the two and a half billion Christians are governed by her doctrines and laws. This is the same religious power that through the dark ages ruled by persecution, torture, and death, as the penalty for disobeying her beliefs. It should be clear that Antichrist is not a man, but secular and religious bodies that have replaced Christ with a false gospel.

17:12 And the ten horns which thou sawest are ten kings, which have received no kingdom as yet; but receive power as kings one hour with the beast.

17:13 These have one mind, and shall give their power and strength unto the beast.

17:14 These shall make war with the Lamb, and the Lamb shall overcome them: for he is Lord of lords, and King of kings: and they that are with him are called, and chosen, and faithful.

17:15 And he saith unto me, The waters which thou sawest, where the whore sitteth, are peoples, and multitudes, and nations, and tongues.

17:16 And the ten horns which thou sawest upon the beast, these shall hate the whore, and shall make her desolate and naked, and shall eat her flesh, and burn her with fire.

17:17 For God hath put in their hearts to fulfil his will, and to agree, and give their kingdom unto the beast, until the words of God shall be fulfilled.

17:18 And the woman which thou sawest is that great city, which reigneth over the kings of the earth.

The ten horns denote the political powers that work with religious powers to control the masses by enforcing the rule of law. Politicians are quick to recognise that religious leaders who hold power over the masses, can be used to their advantage. Likewise religious leaders also use political powers to their ends. The priests in Jesus day took advantage of making sure that Rome knew the accusations they had invented about Jesus. The 'hour' was the short time in which power was given to the religious and political leaders to be single minded in putting Jesus to death by crucifixion. The priests had put their case to the Roman authorities who had no choice but to yield to their wish.

In the Garden of Gethsemane Jesus fought his greatest battle. His anguish was described as 'sweat that looked like blood'. Jesus was aware that what was put in the hearts of his enemies was ordained of God. But the anguish that Jesus had suffered and overcome in the Garden of Gethsemane was an eternal victory for humanity. When Jesus was presented before the Roman Governor, he remarked,

> *'You could have no power at all against me unless it had been given you from above. Therefore the one who delivered me to you has the greater sin'* (John 19:11).

Rome fulfilled God's purpose in more ways than one. The stage was set for all the players to come together at this point in history. It was the fullness of time when Rome had no other option but to give the Jews the jurisdiction to crucify the Son of God. It was entirely up to the Jews to release either Barabbas or Jesus from the sentence of death. It was a choice between setting Jesus free, or setting a thief free, (as was the custom of the day).

Although Jesus' followers were peaceful while spreading the gospel message from Jerusalem to Rome, zealots concerned with Roman occupation had begun wars and skirmishes throughout Israel. The tension with Rome increased and finally ended with the Roman army destroying the centre of their world. This was the day which Daniel had warned of as 'the abomination that makes desolate'. Rome had accomplished what was finally God's judgment on Israel. *'For God hath put in their hearts to fulfil his will'* (Revelation 17:18).

Yet although the physical temple at Jerusalem was finally destroyed, the religion of the Jews of which the laws of Moses were central, remains an important core of Judaic Christianity's teaching to this day. 'The great city' that was the centre of religious teachings still has power over those 'kings' who dominate the religions of Judaism, Judaic Christianity, and to some extent, the religion of Islam, all of which are rooted in the Old Testament law.

Those who claim they are not under law, yet preach that humanity remains in a sinful condition until Jesus returns, should realise that such preaching contradicts what the scriptures teach about God's grace. We cannot have sinful tendencies and belong to the body of Christ, nether can God dwell within an unholy temple. There is a difference between temptations of the flesh and sins of the flesh. Judaic Christianity has compromised the Gospel of Christ by allowing the beastly powers to govern by the rule of law rather than the preaching of Christ. Rarely is there a sermon preached, especially amongst protestant evangelists who remind us of our sinful condition, rather than preaching the knowledge of Christ as 'the truth that sets one free' from fear.

REVELATION 18

18:1   And after these things I saw another angel come down from heaven, having great power; and the earth was lightened with his glory.

18:2   And he cried mightily with a strong voice, saying, Babylon the great is fallen, is fallen, and is become the habitation of devils, and the hold of every foul spirit, and a cage of every unclean and hateful bird.

18:3   For all nations have drunk of the wine of the wrath of her fornication, and the kings of the earth have committed fornication with her, and the merchants of the earth are waxed rich through the abundance of her delicacies.

Jerusalem is here likened to Babylon because the city was becoming more corrupt by the year. Jerusalem was to be a 'light on a hill', 'a city of refuge', where the poor, the hungry, and the sick, could find comfort and hope. Many in Jerusalem and the regions of Judea had become rich through the city's commerce and delicacies while succumbing to the pleasures and luxuries that the city had afforded them. The merchants of the world found Jerusalem a perfect trading partner because of her strategic position within the known world. From Herod's magnificent harbour at Caesarea, approximately sixty miles from Jerusalem, merchants and travellers could easily access the trade route from the port city through the Kedron Valley to Jerusalem.

18:4 And I heard another voice from heaven, saying, Come out of her, my people, that ye be not partakers of her sins, and that ye receive not of her plagues.

18:5 For her sins have reached unto heaven, and God hath remembered her iniquities.

18:6 Reward her even as she rewarded you, and double unto her double according to her works: in the cup which she hath filled fill to her double.

18:7 How much she hath glorified herself, and lived deliciously, so much torment and sorrow give her: for she saith in her heart, I sit a queen, and am no widow, and shall see no sorrow.

18:8 Therefore shall her plagues come in one day, death, and mourning, and famine; and she shall be utterly burned with fire: for strong is the Lord God who judgeth her.

The call for God's people to come out and be separate from the world remains relevant today. Luxury and pleasure have taken precedence over the preservation of the spirit. The lesson here is the assurance that when tragedy strikes there is an escape from the grief we are often called to endure. Almost every other day we hear reports of financial ruin because of man's greed, fear, and insecurity. Whether political, secular or religious, nothing has changed through history. Lust for money and power remain prevalent in all walks of life. Babylon remains symbolic of the world and its temporary pleasures that compel us to accumulate material possessions, rather than spiritual things that remain permanent.

18:9 And the kings of the earth, who have committed fornication and lived deliciously with her, shall bewail her, and lament for her, when they shall see the smoke of her burning,

18:10 Standing afar off for the fear of her torment, saying, Alas, alas that great city Babylon, that mighty city! for in one hour is thy judgment come.

The extent of the fire and smoke that engulfed and destroyed the old city of Jerusalem in 70 AD was seen from those in the ships in the port at Caesarea. Within a short time, Jerusalem was reduced from a glorious city to a place of desolation.

18:11 And the merchants of the earth shall weep and mourn over her; for no man buyeth their merchandise any more:

18:12 The merchandise of gold, and silver, and precious stones, and of pearls, and fine linen, and purple, and silk, and scarlet, and all thyine wood, and all manner vessels of ivory, and all manner vessels of most precious wood, and of brass, and iron, and marble,

18:13 And cinnamon, and odours, and ointments, and frankincense, and wine, and oil, and fine flour, and wheat, and beasts, and sheep, and horses, and chariots, and slaves, and souls of men.

18:14 And the fruits that thy soul lusted after are departed from thee, and all things which were dainty and goodly are departed from thee, and thou shalt find them no more at all.

All that is found in the commercial world cannot buy peace and security. While attending to their commercial and worldly possessions, many believers had lost their first love. Jesus and the Apostles cautioned that the material things we long for do not offer lasting security. Worldly treasures will always deteriorate, but while our bodies of flesh are temporal, the spirit is permanent and belongs to God.

The mention here of 'souls of men' being bought and sold is a reminder that the spirit can only be perfected while it dwells within a body of flesh. The body, mind, and spirit forms the soul (Hebrews 12:23). We are continually being renewed in the 'spirit of the mind', which forms the individual character. The rebirth of the body, mind, and spirit, belongs to God; it cannot be bought and sold. The practice of paying money to release a family member's tormented soul from a fictional place called purgatory continues in many parts of the world to this day .

18:15 The merchants of these things, which were made rich by her, shall stand afar off for the fear of her torment, weeping and wailing,

18:16 And saying, Alas, alas that great city, that was clothed in fine linen, and purple, and scarlet, and decked with gold, and precious stones, and pearls!

18:17 For in one hour so great riches is come to nought. And every shipmaster, and all the company in ships, and sailors, and as many as trade by sea, stood afar off,

18:18 And cried when they saw the smoke of her burning, saying, What city is like unto this great city!

18:19 And they cast dust on their heads, and cried, weeping and wailing, saying, Alas, alas that great city, wherein were made rich all that had ships in the sea by reason of her costliness! for in one hour is she made desolate.

The merchants and ship owners who used the port city of Caesarea witnessed the smoke rising from the ashes of Jerusalem. The realisation that Jerusalem was destroyed along with Herod's temple had a twofold effect on those who saw it burning from afar. The initial shock of the destruction of both the city and temple was one thing, but losing the wealth and power of such a glorious city had an even greater impact. Those who heeded Jesus' and Daniel's words and fled the city were not shaken by this sudden catastrophe because they understood the prophetic warning. This chapter speaks about the Day of Judgment and desolation of Jerusalem because of its disregard of God's grace through Jesus Christ. This was the day in which Jesus and all the prophets killed for their testimony against Israel, were avenged.

18:20 Rejoice over her, thou heaven, and ye holy Apostles and prophets; for God hath avenged you on her.

18:21 And a mighty angel took up a stone like a great millstone, and cast it into the sea, saying, Thus with violence shall that great city Babylon be thrown down, and shall be found no more at all.

18:22 And the voice of harpers, and musicians, and of pipers, and trumpeters, shall be heard no more at all in thee; and no craftsman, of whatsoever craft he be, shall be found any more in thee; and the sound of a millstone shall be heard no more at all in thee;

18:23 And the light of a candle shall shine no more at all in thee; and the voice of the bridegroom and of the bride shall be heard no more at all in thee: for thy merchants were the great men of the earth; for by thy sorceries were all nations deceived.

18:24 And in her was found the blood of prophets, and of saints, and of all that were slain upon the earth.

Forty years previously Jesus had wept when he predicted this day. His first priority was to gather Israel as a hen would gather her chicks, but to no avail.

> *"O Jerusalem, Jerusalem, the one who kills the prophets and stones those who are sent to her! How often I wanted to gather your children together, as a hen gathers her chicks under her wings, but you were not willing!* (Mathew 23:37).

And when he was come near, he beheld the city, and wept over it, Saying, If thou hadst known, even thou, at least in this thy day, the things which belong unto thy peace! but now they are hid from thine eyes. For the days shall come upon thee, that thine enemies shall cast a trench about thee, and compass thee round, and keep thee in on every side, And shall lay thee even with the ground, and thy children within thee; and they shall not leave in thee one stone upon another; because thou knewest not the time of thy visitation (Luke 19:41-44)

Like the prophets before him who were stoned, ridiculed, and killed for their testimony, Jesus suffered the ultimate rejection. Of all the cities in the known world, none were so opposed to the teaching of Jesus as the priests and leaders of Jerusalem. Christians today have much to learn about Jesus' teaching of the Kingdom of God that is already established here on earth. The 'one universal apostolic church' as stated in the Nicene Creed is a far cry from what the 'one universal body of Christ' is. Individuals within their religious faiths, whether Muslim, Jew, Christian, Buddhist or Hindu, and those misguided and restrained within sects and cults, should pay attention to Paul meant by:

There is neither Jew nor Greek, there is neither bond nor free, there is neither male nor female: for ye are all one in Christ Jesus. And if ye be Christ's, then are ye Abraham's seed, and heirs according to the promise (Galatians 3:28, 29).

Revelation 19

19:1 And after these things I heard a great voice of much people in heaven, saying, Alleluia; Salvation, and glory, and honour, and power, unto the Lord our God:

19:2 For true and righteous are his judgments: for he hath judged the great whore, which did corrupt the earth with her fornication, and hath avenged the blood of his servants at her hand.

19:3 And again they said, Alleluia And her smoke rose up for ever and ever.

19:4 And the four and twenty elders and the four beasts fell down and worshipped God that sat on the throne, saying, Amen; Alleluia.

19:5 And a voice came out of the throne, saying, Praise our God, all ye his servants, and ye that fear him, both small and great.

19:6 And I heard as it were the voice of a great multitude, and as the voice of many waters, and as the voice of mighty thunderings, saying, Alleluia: for the Lord God omnipotent reigneth.

19:7 Let us be glad and rejoice, and give honour to him: for the marriage of the Lamb is come, and his wife hath made herself ready.

19:8   And to her was granted that she should be arrayed in fine linen, clean and white: for the fine linen is the righteousness of saints.

19:9   And he saith unto me, Write, Blessed are they which are called unto the marriage supper of the Lamb. And he saith unto me, These are the true sayings of God.

When the mystery of Christ had been revealed to the twenty-four elders, it gave them reason to exclaim 'Alleluia' and 'Amen' as an expression of praise and thankfulness to the Father and Son for the hope they had found in Christ. They realised that although the Jews rejected the power of Jesus' words, a door of faith had been opened to the Gentile nations, represented as 'the voice of a great multitude' that now saw Israel's rejection as the Gentile's blessing. (Romans 11:11,12).

First-century believers rejoiced in the victory that Jesus had won over his enemies. Although the crucifixion had caused much physical pain, Jesus' greatest victory was in overcoming the anguish caused by the rejection and the humiliation he had to endure. He endured the shame and carried the cross even though one of his closest disciple would deny him during those final hours.

Those who heard Jesus' words first-hand realised that the expected messiah was not a fierce warrior who was to wield a physical sword and rule with military might, but one to rule with the 'sword of the spirit' which is the Spirit and Word of truth. The marriage between Christ and the church is likened to a bride and groom that celebrate their union by becoming one flesh.

19:10 And I fell at his feet to worship him. And he said unto me, See thou do it not: I am thy fellowservant, and of thy brethren that have the testimony of Jesus: worship God: for the testimony of Jesus is the spirit of prophecy.

In chapter one, Jesus identifies himself as the *'beginning and the end'*, the *'alpha and the omega'*, the *'first and the last'*, yet here Jesus is speaking of himself simply as a 'fellow servant'. This verse gives a glimpse of the true nature of Jesus as the Son of God. God had breathed into the *first* Adam so that 'the fullness of God' could ultimately dwell within humanity through the sacrifice of the *last* Adam.

That Christ may dwell in your hearts by faith; that ye, being rooted and grounded in love, May be able to comprehend with all saints what is the breadth, and length, and depth, and height; And to know the love of Christ, which passeth knowledge, that ye might be filled with all the fulness of God (Ephesians 3:17-19).

As already observed from Genesis, the first Adam was not in the fullness of God, but rather *'the beginning of the creation of God'*. The Christ of God was manifest within humanity in the fullness of time through natural procreation of the flesh, through the seed of David and finally Joseph, the husband of Mary. The *last* Adam had surrendered his body of flesh so the members of Christ could begin constructing a spiritual temple wherein the fullness of God could dwell forever. Adam, the *'alpha'*, and Jesus, the *'omega'*, had fulfilled all that was ordained before the foundation of the world.

Jesus became a 'servant' and asked not to be worshipped. To worship Jesus as an external god is to ignore the 'indwelling Christ'.

19:11 And I saw heaven opened, and behold a white horse; and he that sat upon him was called Faithful and True, and in righteousness he doth judge and make war.

19:12 His eyes were as a flame of fire, and on his head were many crowns; and he had a name written, that no man knew, but he himself.

19:13 And he was clothed with a vesture dipped in blood: and his name is called The Word of God.

19:14 And the armies which were in heaven followed him upon white horses, clothed in fine linen, white and clean.

19:15 And out of his mouth goeth a sharp sword, that with it he should smite the nations: and he shall rule them with a rod of iron: and he treadeth the winepress of the fierceness and wrath of Almighty God.

19:16 And he hath on his vesture and on his thigh a name written, King Of Kings, And Lord Of Lords.

In this vision we see the followers of Jesus symbolised as members of 'the armies of heaven'. Christ Jesus is here named the Word of God. They are ready to follow Jesus because they are of one mind with Christ. They are clothed in fine linen because they are worthy to proclaim the Word of God to every nation. Jesus has the names 'King of Kings' and 'Lord of Lords' written on his robe and thigh because he brought the Spirit and Word to life. The English word 'Jesus' is not the original Hebrew name, therefore the name Yehoshua, which means 'God is salvation', is not recognized by most Christians. Whenever Jesus spoke, the Spirit and power of the Word reflected his spirit through eyes as a flame of fire. His vesture is dipped in blood to remind humanity of all who had died for their faith and now worthy to wear the figurative white linen, which represents the robe of the righteousness of Christ.

19:17 And I saw an angel standing in the sun; and he cried with a loud voice, saying to all the fowls that fly in the midst of heaven, Come and gather yourselves together unto the supper of the great God;

19:18 That ye may eat the flesh of kings, and the flesh of captains, and the flesh of mighty men, and the flesh of horses, and of them that sit on them, and the flesh of all men, both free and bond, both small and great.

19:19 And I saw the beast, and the kings of the earth, and their armies, gathered together to make war against him that sat on the horse, and against his army.

19:20 And the beast was taken, and with him the false prophet that wrought miracles before him, with which he deceived them that had received the mark of the beast, and them that worshipped his image. These both were cast alive into a lake of fire burning with brimstone.

19:21 And the remnant were slain with the sword of him that sat upon the horse, which sword proceeded out of his mouth: and all the fowls were filled with their flesh.

This scene summarises the time from the beginning of Jesus' ministry to the 'end of all things'. The judgment day had finally fallen on those who were the enemies of Jesus and his followers. Although the beast and false prophet lost the victory, and their identities were now revealed, the spirit of those beastly powers will remain from generation to generation until Christ is acknowledged universally.

'Eating the flesh' shows the completion of the victory over the enemies of Christ. The flesh here represents those who would destroy themselves by their own evil deeds. Jerusalem, like Babylon of old, became a place where the birds of the air had symbolically eaten the corpses of those who had lived only for the desires of the flesh.

REVELATION 20

20:1　And I saw an angel come down from heaven, having the key of the bottomless pit and a great chain in his hand.

20:2　And he laid hold on the dragon, that old serpent, which is the Devil, and Satan, and bound him a thousand years,

20:3　And cast him into the bottomless pit, and shut him up, and set a seal upon him, that he should deceive the nations no more, till the thousand years should be fulfilled: and after that he must be loosed a little season.

The 'dragon', the 'old serpent', the 'Devil' and 'Satan' are synonymous for all who choose the path of evil. Cain, the first murderer, had left a legacy of evil by slaying his brother. The devil and Satan personify individuals in politics, religion, and secular life who pursue their worldly ambitions by using the power of choice to corrupt. People become devils by their own choosing. Cain demonstrated that evil can only be conceived from within one's own mind. Cain was capable of 'ruling over sin' therefore he had only himself to blame for allowing himself to commit murder[4].

In this chapter we are shown symbols of what is first conceived in the mind of the individual, and then from there, the minds of two or more individuals, then to the masses, and then into the consciousness of nations. The dragon, serpent, devil and Satan are symbolic of the

---
4　See comments on Genesis 4:5-10

extent of how far evil may spread. Each cycle of a thousand years is testimony to the rise and fall of figurative devils, demons, dragons, and Satan. We either gather together to form an exclusive body for good, or we gather together to form a body of evil. From there the collective consciousness is a power for good or evil, hence a dragon is in power when evil people or nations collaborate.

20:4 And I saw thrones, and they sat upon them, and judgment was given unto them: and I saw the souls of them that were beheaded for the witness of Jesus, and for the word of God, and which had not worshipped the beast, neither his image, neither had received his mark upon their foreheads, or in their hands; and they lived and reigned with Christ a thousand years.

20:5 But the rest of the dead lived not again until the thousand years were finished. This is the first resurrection.

20:6 Blessed and holy is he that hath part in the first resurrection: on such the second death hath no power, but they shall be priests of God and of Christ, and shall reign with him a thousand years.

The first resurrection was for those amongst Israel who had died with the hope of a better resurrection. The rest of the dead who did not live again until the thousand-year cycle had ended were those amongst the Gentile nations who belonged to Christ. The first resurrection was the promise, first to the Jews, and thereafter to all who would be symbolically adopted into Israel. The Apostle Paul goes to great lengths explaining the role of the Jews and the blessings that the Gentile world had received because of the Jew's rejection of Jesus' message about the Kingdom of God. Regardless of the Jew's rejection of Christ, Paul explicitly states; 'To the Jew first', which means Israel was given the first opportunity to preach Christ rather than law as the means of righteousness (Romans 11. Romans 1:16).

According to the book of Genesis, seven souls, Adam, Seth, Enos, Cainan, Jared, Methuselah and Noah lived for almost one thousand years. (Genesis 5:1-32). The thousand-year cycle ended when the world as it was known was destroyed. Although our life span is now much shorter by comparison, the regeneration of life in Adam's day was within a cycle of a thousand years. A thousand year cycle may seem like a long time to live, let alone sleep for a thousand years, however, whether in death or in sleep, from the time we fall asleep and re-awaken, it is a 'twinkling of an eye'. Each millennium sees the commencement of a new world into which we are re-born and resurrected. Consider the following discourse by Peter when addressing the passing of David and birth of Jesus:

> *Men and brethren, let me freely speak unto you of the patriarch David, that he is both dead and buried, and his sepulchre is with us unto this day. Therefore being a prophet, and knowing that God had sworn with an oath to him, that of the fruit of his loins, according to the flesh, he would raise up Christ to sit on his throne; He seeing this before spake of the resurrection of Christ, that his soul was not left in hell, neither his flesh did see corruption. This Jesus hath God raised up, whereof we all are witnesses. Therefore being by the right hand of God exalted, and having received of the Father the promise of the Holy Ghost, he hath shed forth this, which ye now see and hear. For David is not ascended into the heavens: but he saith himself, The Lord said unto my Lord, Sit thou on my right hand, Until I make thy foes thy footstool. Therefore let all the house of Israel know assuredly, that God hath made the same Jesus, whom ye have crucified, both Lord and Christ. Now when they heard this, they were pricked in their heart, and said unto Peter and to the rest of the Apostles, Men and brethren, what shall we do? Then Peter said unto them, Repent, and be baptized every one of you in the name of Jesus Christ for the remission of sins, and ye shall receive the gift of the Holy Ghost* (Acts 2:29- 38).

The cause of the listeners being 'cut to the heart' was the realisation that the person the Jews had crucified was in fact the resurrected David, the one of whom God spoke of as a 'man after God's own heart' and who was promised not be left in the grave. David was resurrected through the natural procreation of the flesh. Paul could say with confidence that Jesus was born in the natural way (Romans 1:3, 4). In Peter's discourse, we learn just how important it is to have hope beyond the grave. In David, we learn that the true resurrection of life is the rebirth of each soul through procreation of the flesh. Since the time men called upon the Lord, many souls have died for their testimony and faith because they refused to bow down to images or to serve other gods. They willingly went to their deaths with the hope of 'a better resurrection' (Hebrews 11:35). Elijah had appeared again in the spirit of John the Baptist, along with those 'men of Nineveh' who rose again to preach against the evil generation that was the first century (Matthew 11:13, 14; 12:24). Daniel was told to rest until his allotted time when 'many who slept in the dust' would be resurrected to a new life (Daniel 12:2; 12:13).

The Apostle Paul describes it this way:

Behold, I shew you a mystery; We shall not all sleep, but we shall all be changed, In a moment, in the twinkling of an eye, at the last trump: for the trumpet shall sound, and the dead shall be raised incorruptible, and we shall be changed. For this corruptible must put on incorruption, and this mortal must put on immortality. So when this corruptible shall have put on incorruption, and this mortal shall have put on immortality, then shall be brought to pass the saying that is written, Death is swallowed up in victory. O death, where is thy sting? O grave, where is thy victory? The sting of death is sin; and the strength of sin is the law. But thanks be to God, which giveth us the victory through our Lord Jesus Christ. Therefore, my beloved brethren, be ye stedfast, unmoveable, always abounding in the work of the Lord, forasmuch as ye know that your labour is not in vain in the Lord (1 Corinthians 15:51-58).

Many religions believe in re-incarnation, but few understand the meaning of incarnation within the body of Christ. There is a difference between incarnation and re-incarnation. The problem for most people with religious faith is the difficulty in letting go of the person they are now. Most religious people want to see themselves in a new and glorified body in a utopian existence, and in a glorified and immortal body. However, while that may sound comforting, that is not what the scriptures teach about the nature of everlasting life. Our loved ones that have gone before us are in the hearts of the living, but when we are reborn, there is no memory of our former lives. Our ultimate goal is to have the mind of Christ, a mind that extends to those beyond our immediate family. As Jesus said:

For whosoever shall do the will of God, the same is my brother, and my sister, and mother (Mark 3:35)

20:7 And when the thousand years are expired, Satan shall be loosed out of his prison,

20:8 And shall go out to deceive the nations which are in the four quarters of the earth, Gog, and Magog, to gather them together to battle: the number of whom is as the sand of the sea.

20:9 And they went up on the breadth of the earth, and compassed the camp of the saints about, and the beloved city: and fire came down from God out of heaven, and devoured them.

20:10 And the devil that deceived them was cast into the lake of fire and brimstone, where the beast and the false prophet are, and shall be tormented day and night for ever and ever.

It *was time* to destroy the works of the devil, here symbolised as those satanic powers that opposed the teachings of Jesus. Each thousand-year cycle records a significant event that changes the course of history. A thousand years before Jesus was born, David had overcome his enemies by physical force, but now, in the fullness of Christ, his greatest battle was against the forces of evil.

For we wrestle not against flesh and blood, but against principalities, against powers, against the rulers of the darkness of this world, against spiritual wickedness in high places (Ephesians 6:12).

David's battle was not only against the political powers that had once again subjugated his own nation but against those powers that held the nation in bondage to religion and law. Satan is here symbolised as those with the power to plot evil but are prisoners of their own corruption. Throughout history there have been many significant events that have occurred around thousand-year cycles. Adam, Abraham, David and Jesus were separated by a thousand years, while men such as Richard the Lion heart, Saladin, and men like Adolf Hitler, although not specifically related to John's visions, helped to shape world events at each thousand year cycle. For example, a thousand years after the destruction of Jerusalem, the first crusaders freed the city of Jerusalem that was under the rule of Islam. Within the next thousand year cycle, Adolph Hitler, with a close association to the Arab world, may have changed the outcome and course of history had he won the victory. Given that the most dominant religion in the world has its roots in Judaism, it is not unreasonable to suggest that those beastly powers may have attempted to claim Jerusalem as their 'holy city'.

It is interesting that the actual city of Jerusalem, rather than the spiritual city of Jerusalem is at the centre of conflict between Judaism, Islam, and Judaic Christianity. Islam has the Dome of the Rock, Judaism has the Wailing Wall, and Christians have their Armageddon, believed to be the place where the final battle between good and evil will be physically fought.

In the above vision, John was shown that despite evil men destined to dictate and rule by bondage and law, Christ Jesus destroyed all the enemies and gave humanity freedom to worship in spirit and in truth. It was the Word of God that caused the symbolic fire from heaven that destroyed everything the old Jerusalem stood for.

20:11 And I saw a great white throne, and him that sat on it, from whose face the earth and the heaven fled away; and there was found no place for them.

20:12 And I saw the dead, small and great, stand before God; and the books were opened: and another book was opened, which is the book of life: and the dead were judged out of those things which were written in the books, according to their works.

20:13 And the sea gave up the dead which were in it; and death and hell delivered up the dead which were in them: and they were judged every man according to their works.

20:14 And death and hell were cast into the lake of fire. This is the second death.

20:15 And whosoever was not found written in the book of life was cast into the lake of fire.

In this eternal city now called the 'New Jerusalem' no one needs to be born without hope since all may chose to be born within the body of Christ as citizens of a spiritual and permanent city. As discussed in the introduction, Christ is not a person, but rather 'Christ within' that is eternal and within all who have 'fallen asleep'. Only those who ignore their Christ consciousness are subject to a 'second death' and remain outside the body of Christ. We are either alive or dead in Christ during our life time. When it comes to judgment there is no respect of a person's position whether rich or poor. The two books represent two classes of people; those who are alive to Christ, and those who are dead in Christ. The symbolic book of life is the self-fulfilling judgment of all who reject 'the law of the spirit of life that guides our Christ consciousness' (Romans 8:2). The fires of hell describe what we may put ourselves through by choosing a path of evil rather than good.

REVELATION 21

21:1 And I saw a new heaven and a new earth: for the first heaven and the first earth were passed away; and there was no more sea.

21:2 And I John saw the holy city, new Jerusalem, coming down from God out of heaven, prepared as a bride adorned for her husband.

21:3 And I heard a great voice out of heaven saying, Behold, the tabernacle of God is with men, and he will dwell with them, and they shall be his people, and God himself shall be with them, and be their God.

John's vision of the new heavens, new earth, and the new Jerusalem coming down from heaven as 'a bride adorned for her husband', shows there are no borders between the nations and religions of the world symbolised here by 'no more seas' that separate people and nations.

> *Now therefore ye are no more strangers and foreigners, but fellow citizens with the saints, and of the household of God; And are built upon the foundation of the Apostles and prophets, Jesus Christ himself being the chief corner stone; In whom all the building fitly framed together groweth unto an holy temple in the Lord: In whom ye also are builded together for an habitation of God through the Spirit* (Ephesians 2:19-22).

> *And to know the love of Christ, which passeth knowledge, that ye might be filled with all the fullness of God. Now unto him that is able to do exceeding abundantly above all that we ask or think, according to the power that worketh in us, Unto him be glory in the church by Christ Jesus throughout all ages, world without end. Amen* (Ephesians 3:19-21).

No other letter condenses the good news of the gospel as beautifully as Paul's letter to the Ephesians. In just a few pages Paul outlines the completeness of Christ's work and the role of the church. But of more importance, Paul speaks of the 'power' that works within each member that ensures the ongoing construction of God's dwelling place that will continue from generation to generation. Paul is resolute that the Kingdom of God is a present reality. Those within Paul's generation were already 'citizens' that had entered the new Jerusalem. The 'first heaven and the first earth' had passed away when God's gift of grace was given to the world. Paul's expression of 'heavenly things' describes those who remain within heavenly places from generation to generation.

> *And to make all men see what is the fellowship of the mystery, which from the beginning of the world hath been hid in God, who created all things by Jesus Christ: To the intent that now unto the principalities and powers in heavenly places might be known by the church the manifold wisdom of God, According to the eternal purpose which he purposed in Christ Jesus our Lord: In whom we have boldness and access with confidence by the faith of him. Wherefore I desire that ye faint not at my tribulations for you, which is your glory. For this cause I bow my knees unto the Father of our Lord Jesus Christ, Of whom the whole family in heaven and earth is named, That he would grant you, according to the riches of his glory, to be strengthened with might by his Spirit in the inner man; That Christ may dwell in your hearts by faith; that ye, being rooted and grounded in love, May be able to comprehend with all saints what is the breadth, and length, and depth, and height; And to know the love of Christ, which passeth knowledge, that ye might be filled with all the fullness of God* (Ephesians 3:9-19).

John's visions are now coming to a close. Here we see an invitation that had begun almost two thousand years ago to gather together as one banner under Christ. It is an invitation to live in peace and security within the new Jerusalem, here described as the 'the tabernacle of God that is with men'. The invitation is to Israel and the Gentile world, and all who may worship in spirit and truth. The 'body of Christ' should no longer divided by different faiths and religions since all are invited to dwell within the New Jerusalem and tabernacle of God under the banner of Christ.

> *Which in other ages was not made known unto the sons of men, as it is now revealed unto his holy Apostles and prophets by the Spirit; That the Gentiles should be fellowheirs, and of the same body, and partakers of his promise in Christ by the Gospel* (Ephesians 3:5-6).

21:4 And God shall wipe away all tears from their eyes; and there shall be no more death, neither sorrow, nor crying, neither shall there be any more pain: for the former things are passed away.

21:5 And he that sat upon the throne said, Behold, I make all things new. And he said unto me, Write: for these words are true and faithful.

21:6 And he said unto me, It is done. I am Alpha and Omega, the beginning and the end. I will give unto him that is athirst of the fountain of the water of life freely.

21:7 He that overcometh shall inherit all things; and I will be his God, and he shall be my son.

Since God now dwells within the flesh and blood of humanity, there should be no more fear of death. The citizens of the New Jerusalem know that by having the knowledge and wisdom of God, sickness, disease, pain, suffering, and even death, has been deal with. The citizens of the New Jerusalem are aware that because Omniscience is within humanity, sickness and disease will eventually be overcome.

The citizens know that the signs and wonders happening within medicine, is not man alone, but the spirit of omniscience within man. They no longer fear death because they have the assurance that life is eternal through love and procreation. They are forever in the presence of God and embracing what was once feared.

> *That the God of our Lord Jesus Christ, the Father of glory, may give unto you the spirit of wisdom and revelation in the knowledge of him: The eyes of your understanding being enlightened; that ye may know what is the hope of his calling, and what the riches of the glory of his inheritance in the saints, And what is the exceeding greatness of his power to us-ward who believe, according to the working of his mighty power, Which he wrought in Christ, when he raised him from the dead, and set him at his own right hand in the heavenly places, Far above all principality, and power, and might, and dominion, and every name that is named, not only in this world, but also in that which is to come: And hath put all things under his feet, and gave him to be the head over all things to the church, Which is his body, the fullness of him that filleth all in all* (Ephesians 1:17-23).

> *And you hath he quickened, who were dead in trespasses and sins; Wherein in time past ye walked according to the course of this world, according to the prince of the power of the air, the spirit that now worketh in the children of disobedience: Among whom also we all had our conversation in times past in the lusts of our flesh, fulfilling the desires of the flesh and of the mind; and were by nature the children of wrath, even as others* (Ephesians 2:1-3).

21:8 But the fearful, and unbelieving, and the abominable, and murderers, and whoremongers, and sorcerers, and idolaters, and all liars, shall have their part in the lake which burneth with fire and brimstone: which is the second death.

Most of us have been tested both mentally and physically. Our lack of faith, whether in God or in our individual ability to overcome doubt and fear may be likened to fiery trials. Whichever way we look at it, we are strengthened or weakened through our trials for better or for worse through them. Of all the things that beset us, it is self-doubt we must conquer. Unfortunately many do not see that trials and tribulations are for our learning, not only in this life but in the life to come.

Those who continue to have 'fearful' traits can only blame themselves for a 'second death'. The lake which burns with fire and brimstone is an analogy for the life we make for ourselves by remaining 'dead in Christ'. Yet while we can all be cowardly, unbelieving, or abominable, here we see that our attitude towards the trials and tribulations we go through will determine our destiny and place in this world.

> *Beloved, think it not strange concerning the fiery trial which is to try you, as though some strange thing happened unto you: But rejoice, inasmuch as ye are partakers of Christ's sufferings; that, when his glory shall be revealed, ye may be glad also with exceeding joy. If ye be reproached for the name of Christ, happy are ye; for the spirit of glory and of God resteth upon you: on their part he is evil spoken of, but on your part he is glorified. But let none of you suffer as a murderer, or as a thief, or as an evildoer, or as a busybody in other men's matters. Yet if any man suffer as a Christian, let him not be ashamed; but let him glorify God on this behalf. For the time is come that judgment must begin at the house of God: and if it first begin at us, what shall the end be of them that obey not the Gospel of God? And if the righteous scarcely be saved, where shall the ungodly and the sinner appear? Wherefore let them that suffer according to the will of God commit the keeping of their souls to him in well doing, as unto a faithful Creator (1 Peter 4:12-19).*

21:9   And there came unto me one of the seven angels which had the seven vials full of the seven last plagues, and talked with me, saying, Come hither, I will shew thee the bride, the Lamb's wife.

21:10 And he carried me away in the spirit to a great and high mountain, and shewed me that great city, the holy Jerusalem, descending out of heaven from God,

> **21:11** Having the glory of God: and her light was like unto a stone most precious, even like a jasper stone, clear as crystal;

By comparison all the earthly kingdoms that have come and gone could not compare with the Kingdom of God revealed in the hearts and minds of all who believe. Therefore Jesus was compelled to say, when tempted to embrace the things of this world, *'It is written, You shall worship the Lord your God, and Him only you shall serve'* (Matthew 4:10).

Jesus' mission was to accomplish the Father's will by recreating not a New Jerusalem under the law, but a spiritual and permanent city without boundaries or rules. Had Eve chosen not to partake from the tree of the knowledge of good and evil, and had remained innocent of her nakedness, there would have been no way to bring the fullness of Christ into the world, nor a way for God to dwell amongst humanity. The figurative 'bride of Christ' is the marriage between humanity and God represented by the body of Christ. The one true church is the tabernacle of God now with men, a continuous construction being built from precious living stones that are the members of Christ.

> *Wherefore laying aside all malice, and all guile, and hypocrisies, and envies, and all evil speakings, As newborn babes, desire the sincere milk of the word, that ye may grow thereby: If so be ye have tasted that the Lord is gracious. To whom coming, as unto a living stone, disallowed indeed of men, but chosen of God, and precious, Ye also, as lively stones, are built up a spiritual house, an holy priesthood, to offer up spiritual sacrifices, acceptable to God by Jesus Christ. Wherefore also it is contained in the scripture, Behold, I lay in Sion a chief corner stone, elect, precious: and he that believeth on him shall not be confounded. Unto you therefore which believe he is precious: but unto them which be disobedient, the stone which the builders disallowed, the same is made the head of the corner, And a stone of stumbling, and a rock of offence, even to them which stumble at the word, being disobedient: whereunto also they were appointed. But ye are a chosen generation, a royal priesthood, an holy nation, a*

peculiar people; that ye should shew forth the praises of him who hath called you out of darkness into his marvellous light; Which in time past were not a people, but are now the people of God: which had not obtained mercy, but now have obtained mercy (1 Peter 2:1-10).

The stone in John's vision is like jasper and is 'as clear as crystal' because it allows the light to illuminate the stone. All the precious stones that make up the foundation of the spiritual city become one precious stone represented by members of the body of Christ and illuminated with the Spirit and Word of God.

21:12 And had a wall great and high, and had twelve gates, and at the gates twelve angels, and names written thereon, which are the names of the twelve tribes of the children of Israel:

21:13 On the east three gates; on the north three gates; on the south three gates; and on the west three gates.

21:14 And the wall of the city had twelve foundations, and in them the names of the twelve Apostles of the Lamb.

The restoration of spiritual Israel is an important theme of the gospels and Epistles. The number twelve typifies the importance of the twelve tribes from where a remnant remains protected with a high wall. There is no excuse for any nation of the world to say they cannot see the city since the walls are transparent. Neither is there an excuse for anyone not to enter through any one of the twelve gates from where all from any nation of the world may enter from any direction, whether North, South, East, or West. John's vision leaves no doubt this city will never crumble or lie in ruins since it has twelve separate foundations.

21:15 And he that talked with me had a golden reed to measure the city, and the gates thereof, and the wall thereof.

21:16 And the city lieth foursquare, and the length is as large as the breadth: and he measured the city with the reed, twelve thousand furlongs. The length and the breadth and the height of it are equal.

21:17 And he measured the wall thereof, an hundred and forty and four cubits, according to the measure of a man, that is, of the angel.

The measurements of the base, length, and height of the city compared to 'the measure of a man' shows the significance of the scale of a man compared to the volume of space within the city. There is no limit to the number of citizens who occupy the city. The number one hundred and forty four thousand again signifies an unlimited number. Twelve times twelve represents those amongst the twelve tribes of Israel that are redeemed. The number twelve multiplied by the same number is a reminder that the city may hold an innumerable number. Whether one hundred and forty four, one hundred and forty four thousand, or one hundred and forty four million, the number one hundred and forty four represents the unlimited redeemed who are here likened to 'angels' because they are wearing the white robes that represent the righteousness of Christ. The city is protected by its high walls so the only way to enter is through its gates.

21:18 And the building of the wall of it was of jasper: and the city was pure gold, like unto clear glass.

21:19 And the foundations of the wall of the city were garnished with all manner of precious stones. The first foundation was jasper; the second, sapphire; the third, a chalcedony; the fourth, an emerald;

21:20 The fifth, sardonyx; the sixth, sardius; the seventh, chrysolyte; the eighth, beryl; the ninth, a topaz; the tenth, a chrysoprasus; the eleventh, a jacinth; the twelfth, an amethyst.

21:21 And the twelve gates were twelve pearls: every several gate was of one pearl: and the street of the city was pure gold, as it were transparent glass.

Jasper is as clear as crystal and likened to the glorious light that matches polished gold so the city is not hidden behind its walls. The figurative spiritual city is open to all nations and people who enter, as there is no discrimination between nations and people under God. The twelve Apostles of Israel are the foundations of the city. The Apostles are likened to precious stones which differ from one another. The foundations are above-ground so all may see and be inspired by what Jesus and the Apostles have given to the world.

The single pearl that represents each gate denotes the value placed on each soul that enters the city. The streets of gold, unlike the red carpet that many dignitaries expect, are for those who have won the victory over the world and now dwell within 'heavenly places'.

21:22 And I saw no temple therein: for the Lord God Almighty and the Lamb are the temple of it.

21:23 And the city had no need of the sun, neither of the moon, to shine in it: for the glory of God did lighten it, and the Lamb is the light thereof.

21:24 And the nations of them which are saved shall walk in the light of it: and the kings of the earth do bring their glory and honour into it.

21:25 And the gates of it shall not be shut at all by day: for there shall be no night there.

21:26 And they shall bring the glory and honour of the nations into it.

21:27 And there shall in no wise enter into it anything that defileth, neither whatsoever worketh abomination, or maketh a lie: but they which are written in the Lamb's book of life.

The dwelling place of God is now permanently within this world. It cannot be overstated that the temple of God resides within humanity. It does not need light from the sun or moon because the knowledge of Christ has illuminated each precious stone on which the temple is built. The members of the house of God belong to Christ; hence the church cannot be defiled. The mystery of Christ has been revealed through the gospels; therefore the nations are invited to bring their glory and honour into the New Jerusalem.

REVELATION 22

22:1 And he shewed me a pure river of water of life, clear as crystal, proceeding out of the throne of God and of the Lamb.

22:2 In the midst of the street of it, and on either side of the river, was there the tree of life, which bare twelve manner of fruits, and yielded her fruit every month: and the leaves of the tree were for the healing of the nations.

22:3 And there shall be no more curse: but the throne of God and of the Lamb shall be in it; and his servants shall serve him:

22:4 And they shall see his face; and his name shall be in their foreheads.

22:5 And there shall be no night there; and they need no candle, neither light of the sun; for the Lord God giveth them light: and they shall reign forever and ever.

While the book of Genesis speaks of a single river that flowed out of Eden and divided into four rivers that watered the earth, in this vision, John sees just one crystal clear river. The tree of life is central with its branches overhanging either side of the river so the nations may partake of its fruits month by month. The tree of life is symbolic not only of the gifts of procreation, but also for the gift of never ending life through the fruits of love and procreation.

The tree of the knowledge of good and evil cannot be separated from the tree of life. Since from the beginning both trees were in the centre of the garden and shared a single trunk with one purpose (Genesis 2:9. Genesis 3:3). Without the knowledge of good and evil, the tree of life would be meaningless. Both trees share one truth, and that truth is the inseparable link between life, death, and the regeneration of life through each family tree with its several branches. There is no longer the command 'do not taste, do not touch', because the law has been fulfilled (Genesis3:2, 3). The tree of life is no longer guarded because procreation is no longer restricted within the presence of God, as it was in the Garden of Eden. Only since Eve partook from the tree of the knowledge of good and evil that she was aware of her nakedness and desire to procreate. Eve hid from the presence of God because procreation was forbidden in the Garden of Eden.

The light that was from the beginning is the light of Christ. The division of the light from the darkness occurred before the sun, moon, and stars had appeared on the 4th day. A million candles would add nothing to the light of Christ.

There is no more 'curse' because work, toil and sweat take on a different meaning. Work was not cursed back in the days of Adam, but the earth was cursed for man's sake. Those who prefer not to work and have idle time on their hands are missing out on the blessings that are the fruits of labour. Toiling amongst the thorns and thistles with hard work and sweat is often rewarded with better health and longer life.

22:6   And he said unto me, These sayings are faithful and true: and the Lord God of the holy prophets sent his angel to shew unto his servants the things which must shortly be done.

22:7   Behold, I come quickly: blessed is he that keepeth the sayings of the prophecy of this book.

The words are a blessing because 'the prophecy of this book' is the certainty that Christ will be revealed to all. John's visions are 'words that are faithful and true' and not words that subject the believer to fear about the future. 'Behold I am coming quickly' is repeated here to remind the reader of what was about to take place in the first century. John's visions were a comfort and strength to those who were about to go through the most significant event in history. Judgment day was about to fall upon Jerusalem and its inhabitants, and thus it was essential that believers were at peace with themselves through the knowledge and revelation of Christ.

22:8 And I John saw these things, and heard them. And when I had heard and seen, I fell down to worship before the feet of the angel which shewed me these things.

22:9 Then saith he unto me, See thou do it not: for I am thy fellowservant, and of thy brethren the prophets, and of them which keep the sayings of this book: worship God.

22:10 And he saith unto me, Seal not the sayings of the prophecy of this book: for the time is at hand.

22:11 He that is unjust, let him be unjust still: and he which is filthy, let him be filthy still: and he that is righteous, let him be righteous still: and he that is holy, let him be holy still.

22:12 And, behold, I come quickly; and my reward is with me, to give every man according as his work shall be.

The angel who asks not to be worshipped is the same angel who had said; 'And behold, I am coming quickly, and my reward is with me'. There is a difference between bowing before a king or queen and worshipping a king or queen. Once again John is reminded of the revelation of Christ as something that was imminent; therefore the words of this book that reveal the finished work of Christ must not be sealed. This scene bids one to ask; if the time was at hand in the days of the Apostles, why do the opposite and seal the words by teaching that the end time is still in the future?

22:13 I am Alpha and Omega, the beginning and the end, the first and the last.

22:14 Blessed are they that do his commandments, that they may have right to the tree of life, and may enter in through the gates into the city.

22:15 For without are dogs, and sorcerers, and whoremongers, and murderers, and idolaters, and whosoever loveth and maketh a lie.

22:16 I Jesus have sent mine angel to testify unto you these things in the churches. I am the root and the offspring of David, and the bright and morning star.

When the prophecy about the destruction of Jerusalem was finally fulfilled, there was a misunderstanding about the nature of the coming and appearance of Christ. The end of the world was never intended to be a global cataclysmic event with a physical Jesus and a host of angels descending from the heavens with literal lightning, earthquakes, and trumpet sounds. The 'appearance' or 'coming of Christ' was, and remains, a *'revelation'*. It was given to the believers two thousand years ago and remains relevant today to all who embrace 'the faith of Jesus'. The revelation of Christ is likened to 'brightness as lightning that shines from east to west' to those who understand the difference between what is spiritual and what is literal.

The time of the end was the time when the New Jerusalem was resurrected from out of the ashes of the old Jerusalem and transformed into a spiritual city. The gates of the New Jerusalem were opened almost two thousand years ago, with the invitation to all people of all nations to enter. Those who continue to practise sorcery, sexual immorality, murder, idolatry, and lying, are excluded from partaking from the tree of life because they are not 'alive to Christ'. Those evil religious and political leaders that cause suffering, torment, and death, are here described as less than human and remain outside the walls of the New Jerusalem.

Jesus is here called the root and offspring of David, the Bright and Morning Star, because he existed before and after David as the first and last Adam. This last chapter of the Bible reiterates the truth about procreation and the incarnation of Adam, David and Jesus. Through 'the seed of David, according to the flesh' the fullness of Christ was revealed. David was chosen to be raised again in the fullness of Christ and to be exalted as King as promised. David's genuine heartfelt repentance earned him the respect of the Father, who spoke of him as a man after God's own heart :

And when he had removed him, he raised up unto them David to be their king; to whom also he gave their testimony, and said, I have found David the son of Jesse, a man after mine own heart, which shall fulfil all my will (Acts 13: 22-23a).

Again speaking of Jesus:

Then said I, Lo, I come (in the volume of the book it is written of me,) to do thy will, O God (Hebrews 10:7).

The child Jesus is named the Root and the Offspring of David, since he was the 'Son of God' and firstborn of creation named Adam. It was through the blood of the descendants of Adam that the promised seed would be manifest to the world. Jesus, the first and last Adam is therefore named 'the alpha and the omega', 'the root and the offspring of David'.

Within the life of David is demonstrated the rebirth and redemption of all whose sins are forgiven. David was confident that he would not be left in the grave but would be resurrected in the fullness of Christ and exalted as a spiritual King over the new and spiritual Jerusalem (Acts 2:25-37). We may escape the penalty for our sins in this life, but we cannot escape our own self-fulfilling judgment. The Old Testament book of Psalms is a testimony to David's foreknowledge that he would be raised again to fulfil the Father's will.

My God, my God, why hast thou forsaken me? why art thou so far from helping me, and from the words of my roaring? O my God, I cry in the day time, but thou hearest not; and in the night season, and am not silent (Psalm 22:1-2).

Jesus uttered similar words the night before, and on the day of his crucifixion. In his grief, although reminded of the past and present, it was the future that was at stake. The Magi who came from the East knew the Christ child would be born through the seed of David. The 'Root' and the 'Offspring' of David was fulfilled when, in the fullness of time, Immanuel, that is 'God is with us' appeared in Bethlehem, the City of David. David's rebirth was the true resurrection of life. Notice how Paul ties in Jesus birth with the resurrection of life.

Concerning his Son Jesus Christ our Lord, which was made of the seed of David according to the flesh; And declared to be the Son of God with power, according to the spirit of holiness, by the resurrection from the dead (Romans 1:3,4).

22:17 And the Spirit and the bride say, Come. And let him that heareth say, Come. And let him that is athirst come. And whosoever will, let him take the water of life freely.

Jesus had explained to a woman he met at a well that unless she drank from the true fountain of life, she would always be thirsty. When the woman realised what was meant by 'the water of life', she ran back to her village to share what she had learned about the true water of life. But the most striking part of the discourse with the Samaritan woman was how Jesus made the point:

But the hour cometh, and now is, when the true worshippers shall worship the Father in spirit and in truth: for the Father seeketh such to worship him. God is a Spirit: and they that worship him must worship him in spirit and in truth (John 4:23-24).

22:18 For I testify unto every man that heareth the words of the prophecy of this book, If any man shall add unto these things, God shall add unto him the plagues that are written in this book:

22:19 And if any man shall take away from the words of the book of this prophecy, God shall take away his part out of the book of life, and out of the holy city, and from the things which are written in this book.

The finished work of Jesus Christ is the central theme of the 'words of the book of this prophecy'. The 'revelation' of Christ is central not only to John's visions throughout this book, but also central to the writings of Paul and the Apostles. The gospels and Epistles are clear that everything spoken of and relevant to what was 'near' and even 'at the door', had been fulfilled. There is not a single word or prophecy within John's revelation of Jesus Christ that can be added.

22:20 He which testifieth these things saith, Surely I come quickly. Amen. Even so, come, Lord Yeshua.

22:21 The grace of our Lord Yeshua Christ be with you all. Amen.

The last verse of the Bible once again reminds the reader that what was about to take place was to happen 'quickly', therefore nothing was to be added to the finished work of Christ Jesus. Each thousand years marks a new world with mankind drawing closer to the knowledge and revelation of Christ. Beasts, devils, false prophets and dragons are symbolic of evil individuals outside the city who will continue to subdue people and nations with senseless ideologies through philosophers, misguided political leaders, and false prophets that breed useless religions and bigots. Evil will eventually be overcome through the revelation of Christ that will finally see the world sharing in one faith.

> *That Christ may dwell in your hearts by faith; that ye, being rooted and grounded in love, May be able to comprehend with all saints what is the breadth, and length, and depth, and height; And to know the love of Christ, which passeth knowledge, that ye might be filled with all the fullness of God. Now unto him that is able to do exceeding abundantly above all that we ask or think, according to the power that worketh in us, Unto him be glory in the church by Christ Yeshua throughout all ages, world without end. Amen* (Ephesians 3:17-21).

A butterfly rested upon a flower, carefree was he and light as a flake
And there he met a caterpillar sobbing as though his heart would break.
It hurt the happy butterfly to see the caterpillar cry.

Said he whatever is the matter? And may I help in any way?
"I've lost my brother," wept the other, "He's been unwell for many a day;
Now I discover, sad to tell, He's only a dead and empty shell."

"Unhappy grub, be done with weeping, your sickly brother is not dead;
His body's stronger and no longer crawls like a worm, but flies instead.
He dances through the sunny hours and drinks sweet nectar from the flowers."

"Away, away, deceitful villain, go to the winds where you belong,
I won't be grieving at your leaving, so take away your lying tongue,
Am I a foolish slug or snail, to swallow such a fairy tale?

"I'll prove my words, you unbeliever, now listen well and look at me.
I am none other than your brother, alive and fancy free.
Soon you'll be with me in the skies, among the flitting butterflies."

"Ah!" cried the mournful caterpillar, "It's clear I must be seeing things,
You're only a specter sipping nectar, flicking your ornamental wings,
And talking nonsense by the yard, I will not hear another word."

The butterfly gave up the struggle. "I have" he said, "no more to say"
He spread his splendid wings and ascended into the air and flew away.
And while he fluttered far and wide, the caterpillar sat and cried.

G.Eustace Owen

www.ingramcontent.com/pod-product-compliance
Lightning Source LLC
Chambersburg PA
CBHW071604080526
44588CB00010B/1018